Lovers

Unmasked

J. R. Jesse

Publishers Notes

This publication is intended to provide helpful and informative material. It is not intended to diagnose, treat, cure, or prevent any health problem or condition, nor is intended to replace the advice of a physician. No action should be taken solely on the contents of this book. Always consult your physician or qualified health-care professional on any matters regarding your health and before adopting any suggestions in this book or drawing inferences from it.

The author and publisher specifically disclaim all responsibility for any liability, loss or risk, personal or otherwise, which is incurred as a consequence, directly or indirectly, from the use or application of any contents of this book.

© 2014

Manufactured in the United States of America

About The Author

J.R. Jesse was moved to write this book after witnessing his sister's experience in a relationship that became abusive. He deconstructed that relationship based on principles from anthropology and engineering.

Jesse hopes that this information will help prevent abuse as well as encourage men to play key roles in the safe and successful extractions of women trapped in violent situations, along with their children and animals.

Contents

1 A Brother's Perspective

I believe there comes a time in every person's life when they either become willing to deal or they miss the chance to progress as a human being. To be willing to deal can involve having to grapple in order to have impact or to render help.

A single occurrence of abuse I witnessed between my younger sister and her husband was a far bigger turning point for me than I grasped at the time. I failed to deal then, so I missed a chance to render help to someone I love because I didn't want to make anyone uncomfortable.

If I've learned nothing else in my 41 years, I've learned that to look deeply at relationship, you have to be willing to get uncomfortable because relationship is the biggest and most complex thing we do. When that relationship is pathological, the willingness to get uncomfortable might just make the difference between existing and living, or between life and death.

The man my sister married appeared to be just right for her. We all liked him. We are ranching people, we don't go in for any kind of pretense, which is why what Gregory pulled on us and got away with still sickens us. Growing up on a ranch packs a lot of life lessons into the daily rhythms of working with the land, animals and the elements. When it's just you and the crop or you and the weather, reality has a way of separating the wheat from the chaff and it is absolute.

Growing up in this environment Donna was formed into a woman with a strong back, a clean mind and a pure heart. Gregory was a man's man, competent in his business, comfortable in his own skin, easy going, able to laugh at himself, humble, well informed, no substance use, no rough edges, no skeletons in his closet.

The only thing that required any kind of mental adjustment for any of us was the speed with which it all happened. I know what that can mean now, but back then, I didn't. We all chalked it up to true love, besides Donna didn't do any of things that would bring her to the attention of an unscrupulous man.

Gregory got a look at her one evening at a dinner party and set his sights on her. He wanted the whole package: the girl, the career she was building, the relationships she had, the animals she loved, the passions she pursued, the personal best she worked to improve, the happiness she found in simple things, the hopes and dreams she had for the rest of her life. What man wouldn't want to journey through life with a woman who had so much to give? It seemed like a fit.

The speed of it added to the thrill of it. I had never seen Donna so gone over a guy. I figured she had found the love of her life.

Gregory had Donna's parents, siblings, in-laws, nieces and nephews looking him over. I want to stress that nobody had any misgivings about him. Nobody.

All that changed when I visited them after a business trip in May. Shortly after their wedding, Gregory had whisked her away to his mountain home in Montana. We did not know then that isolation is one of the strategies of an abusive partner. We did notice the decline in communication the first year of marriage, but hey, there were newlyweds. In the 23-month interim, they had only visited us once, so we had little "access" and no other information to go on. Later, I would learn this was another part of standard operating procedure for abusive relationships.

The week of my business trip to Montana was mild and sunny. I had meant to call ahead and let them know I'd be in Billings, but as fate would have it, I did not. When I finished my last meeting that Friday afternoon, I just decided to drive out toward their place and surprise them. When I was about 20 minutes away, I stopped at a restaurant and called the house. Gregory answered. If he was uncomfortable about my spur-of-the-minute visit, he didn't show it. I suggested dinner, to which he replied with gusto, "Great! Love to."

When they got there an hour later, I watched from the bar as he steered Donna to the front door. She smiled when she saw me, but it was not a real smile, it was just her mouth, her eyes were not smiling. When I hugged her she felt like a quivering little bird. I couldn't tell how thin she was from looking at her because of her clothing, but I could feel it.

The first primal impression burned into me but instead of calling it, I got sucked into the unspoken protocol of being around a controlling person: acting as if. I acted as if everything was normal.

Dinner was a grueling exercise of cat and mouse as I tried to engage with Donna only to be met with banter from Gregory. She listened attentively to both of us, nodded her head and pushed the food around on her plate, but she didn't make much eye contact and although she talked, she said nothing of substance. By the middle of the meal, I realized I was in the middle of something but I didn't know what. Who was this woman who looked like my sister? I wanted to lean across the table, grab her arm and ask, "Donna, what has happened to you? Are you in there? Are you alright?"

As if he'd read my mind, Gregory clapped her on the back and said she was tired from cleaning the garage that week. His gesture did nothing to relieve my concern. I was sitting across the table from my little sister and there was no doubt that she was not alright. My mind ran through various possibilities, pregnancy, cancer, stroke, accident. As dinner wore on, I began to notice little things, like Gregory telling her what to order and telling her how to eat. This didn't fit with who I knew Donna to be. She was a shadow of herself, literally and figuratively.

Something primal kicks in when threat is sensed. Anyone who contends with it, can tell you how dealing with life and death circumstances alters sensory perception. My inner radar was blaring. I didn't know the story, I certainly didn't know the details, but I knew two things: my sister was not alright and her husband had something to do with that.

Once when he reached in front of her, she flinched. It was just a little flinch and she tried to cover it by pretending to cough, but I caught it. That was all the confirmation I needed.

I had trouble concentrating on his monologues because I was thinking about how much I wanted to get him in the alley behind the restaurant and show him in the most direct manner possible what I thought of his effect on my sister.

If he had been a normal person, he would have realized that he was busted, but he didn't. This is just the tip of the iceberg in terms of how big a role denial plays in these types of relationships. I still did not know what I was seeing and feeling, but I knew something was profoundly wrong and I knew Donna needed help. They didn't invite me to stay the night at their house and it was Gregory that didn't want to get together again the next day, but I insisted.

I went back to my hotel, called my wife, my other sister, Katie and my best friend. (My brother was out of the country.) Everyone dropped what they were doing and went into research mode online, which was overwhelming and confusing. About midnight, Katie thought to call a women's shelter; this was the door we'd been looking for.

Katie debriefed us on some of the fundamentals of domestic violence while we tried to wrap our heads around the unreality of it all. The more she talked, the clearer it became that Donna was being abused by Gregory and that the shell of a woman I had seen earlier that evening was the result of almost two years of that abuse. We were all in agreement that some sort of intervention needed to be staged so that she could be offered a break from the situation. My other brother-in-law, who is a pilot and my buddy got on board to be back up. The two of them and their two grown sons flew up the next morning in a neighbor's plane. (Thank you Harry.)

We followed extrication guidelines (Extrication Guidelines!) from the women's shelter. One of those was to call for a police stand-by to mitigate violence. So, at the appointed time, a police cruiser appeared and parked 50 feet or so down from their driveway. My back-up team pulled up in a rental car behind him. We'd made a simple plan, now it was up to us to pull it off.

Rather than go through any more charades, I showed up early to throw Gregory off balance and see if I could get a few minutes alone with my sister. He fumbled a bit, but got his bearings and began to take charge of the situation. I took out my cell phone, looked him in the eye and pushed a button. The energy in the room changed at once. I walked over to Donna and asked her if she would like to come with me, and that if so, to get what she needed, that I would wait for her. I held her gaze and felt like I was looking into the eyes of a starving child. In the seconds it took to do this, Gregory recovered and ordered her upstairs. I held up my hand to him knowing that this would either confuse him or unleash a monster. Three loud raps at the door took us all by surprise, to my relief, I could see four large silhouettes through the glass on the front door.

Men like Gregory are used to calling the shots. In a sick sense, they've earned it by abusing their woman to the point that she cannot challenge him or will no longer resist him. When tyrants encounter resistance, they tend to go berzerk, which is more or less what Gregory began to do. Before he tried to chase Donna upstairs, he started ordering us all out of his house.

The police cruiser pulled into the driveway at this point and the officer walked up to the front door, which was somehow open. Gregory was in full roar, raging like a mad bull and not knowing who to attack first. I kept telling myself that this only needed to last long enough for Donna to get her things and come back down the stairs. I think having the police there gave us a safety net because it kept Gregory from completely losing control. At last Donna came downstairs with a small suitcase, a cat carrier and a skinny dog on a leash. When Gregory lunged for her, the dog snarled and the four of us stepped forward in unison to block him. Donna's walk behind us to and through the front door seemed to occur in slow motion. Once he realized she was walking out of the house, he turned his wrath on her spewing out things I have never heard a man say to a woman. If I had not been so full of adrenalin, I could have dropped to my knees and cried because I knew that this was what Donna had been listening to for God-knows-how-long. I drove Donna and her animals back home. She sat with her dog curled up in her lap looking out the window like she was in a trance. It felt like I was riding with three skeletons. Apparently Gregory punished her by withholding food from her pets. I learned later that his tirades often occurred over dinner, which negated her desire for food.

Back at the ranch, Katie had the grim task of talking to our parents to prepare them for Donna's arrival. By the time we got there, they had got a hold of themselves. Mom had cried it out and Dad had thought it through. They received her without drama and their own needs in check. Donna was in a fragile state, so our joint purpose was to give her the protection she needed and the space she wanted. After "hellos" (she didn't want hugs) I took her to the bunkhouse that had been fixed up for her. I noticed that Dad had installed double-key deadbolts on all the doors and movement-sensor lights around the roof perimeter.

We were all glad that she'd had the presence of mind to bring her cat and dog because they rallied first and it encouraged all of us during the first few weeks when it was touch and go. Gregory's calls and emails began immediately. He did everything he could to win her back and there were some very tense times when we thought he was going to succeed, but somehow he didn't. When he realized he didn't control her anymore, he became vicious and threatening. This went on for seven months.

Donna spent most of her time alone and slowly began to come up to the house to talk to Mom. It was my dad who took it the hardest. Donna was the baby and she had spent the most time with him during childhood because the ranch by then, was humming like a well-oiled machine. She rode in the saddle with him when she was a toddler and then rode alongside when she was big enough to ride alone. Many evenings when Mom called us in for dinner, the last two in would be Dad and Donna. We would wait to see their silhouettes come up over the horizon riding side by side. Sometimes their horses would simply walk back to the barn, sometimes they would gallop. This was something we never tired of seeing. I knew all of this was working on my dad. Here was a man who could gentle a horse, coax a calf, comfort his wife and set an example for his children, but he did not know what to do to help his youngest daughter through the darkness. He and my mother aged 10 years almost overnight.

Abuse is one of those "elephants in the room." It is there, it is big, but no one knows what it is or what to do even though they are all, in their own way, being crushed by its weight. We have all looked back many times and wondered if we'd jumped out of our seats, or jumped on a plane earlier, if it would have made a difference. None of us know and all of us are haunted by the fact of our own ignorance and what it cost Donna and us.

She still lives on the ranch, she is healing and doing better, but she is not the same person she was before. She was used and abused to the point of being infected with a lot of cruel and perverted ideas about herself and the world. She lost all confidence in herself. The things that a sick person can do are unbelievable until you see them do it or you see the results.

One evening, my dad saddled two horses and asked if she wanted to go for a ride. She shook her head. My mother stood up, pointed to the door and told her to "go get on that horse."

So, she did and an evening tradition was born. More than any other single thing, her evening rides began to bring her back to life. It also did wonders for my dad. Horses. Of course.

This book has been a mission for me. I hope someone finds it worth reading. I hope it will do two things: impress upon readers that domestic violence happens to good women and that other men can play a key role in getting women out of these soul-killing situations.

I work as an engineer making things work, but I have always been interested in how and why people do what they do. Without planning to, I deconstructed my sister's marriage to see what I could learn about its "machinery." I worked from what Donna told me, what other family members told me and from what I witnessed. It was mind-blowing.

Most of the information in this book comes directly from our family's experience. My parents collected clippings about other cases. The anthropologist in me drew from them to write the two relationship compilations. Donna's therapist and social worker reviewed the manuscript to make sure I didn't give any advice or convey any inaccurate information. I have not written Donna's story, but with her permission, I have recorded what we all learned about abuse from our different vantage points.

With the court system as it is, there is little we can do as a nation to adequately address the presence of men like Gregory. They roam the world leaving a trail of destruction behind them because they know how to keep from breaking the law as they break women. But there is something much greater we can do as individuals, we can learn the modus operandi of these human predators to protect ourselves and when possible, we can expose them to protect others. Exposure is the thing they dread above all else. Remember that.

Because Gregory never hit Donna and because she never went to the hospital after the times he raped her, there were no grounds for pursuing criminal action against him. His brief but brutal sojourn through our family has taken a toll on all of us. I now know what it feels like to want to kill someone to protect someone else but to have to choose not to because of the likely legal consequences.

Donna is worth what we have gone through. I think her near-destruction has made us all realize what a gift life is but also how quickly it can be damaged when trust is misplaced. Trust is a big part of the big picture here. This has been a highly impactful lesson for our children, who now have a lot more to work with than their peers in this regard. They have learned some of the warning signs and they have seen the damage done.

Julius Caesar is said to have written something like: the person who will hurt you the most, will be the one you least expect would ever do so.

There are no guarantees in this life, but a measure of wisdom can go a long way in keeping monsters away. I hope this little book might play a role in that for you. Live well!

2 The Quest

After she had recovered from the extraction, Donna had a lot of questions. She knew she was looking for something, but she didn't know what it was or where she would find it. She wanted to know:

• why had he picked her?
• how did he know how to con her?
• why hadn't she been able to see through him?
• what made him the way he is?
• was something wrong with her, too?
• what did she need to know to avoid a repeat experience?

While she was married, she tried many things to placate her husband and heal the relationship—all to no avail. During the last year of the marriage, she began to feel there was something not quite human about her husband. Later, she became sure of it although she did not know anything about evil at the time.

As I watched from a distance and did my own processing, one of the territories I found was personality. It has much to do with why someone pretends to be something they are not; why a lover wears masks, what his masks say about him, what his masks mean to his partner, how he chooses her, why she falls for the masks and where it all leads.

Self expression plays a key role in self image, which is the basis of just about everything that happens to us. It is the sum total of what we think about ourselves, our subconscious marching orders. Self image influences the outcomes of our activities and relationships. When personality is inhibited, self image is diminished and things go can go awry in a big way.

Personality works like this in relationship. For example, when a personality-disordered man meets a personality-inhibited woman, and there is some chemical attraction, the stage can be set for abuse and violence. Abuse and violence come in many forms, some of the worst of which never leaves a mark on anyone although it inflicts deep wounds.

The subconscious mind and the conscious mind are both involved in personality and self image, so is the central nervous system. Working together, they are powerful mechanisms. The most potent of which is the subconscious mind, the repository of experience and information impressed with emotion. The subconscious mind does not have an agenda other than to run its programming, regardless of whether that programming helps or hinders. The conscious mind is the door to the subconscious mind.

There are many irresistible forces in play when two people come together in a way that leads to intimate relationship. When that relationship becomes abusive, it's hard to see and understand that turning unless you know what to look for. In the beginning, there is often a vague sense of something being off, but as statistics show, that is rarely enough to dissuade either person from pursuing the relationship. Once both people are "activated" (by personality), primal emotions kick in and soon they are propelled forward until they are joined like a key in a lock or a hand in a glove.

Even though our personality expression and self image are programmed by experience, we are not stuck with that programming. The self image is key to personality and behavior, but it can be changed and when it changes, so do personality and behavior. This applies whether the programming is positive or negative. Women who have endured different types of mistreatment have said that the most long-lasting was verbal abuse because it changed how they thought of themselves. In the words of a wise woman I know, the verbal abuse "got into" them because of the repetition and reprogrammed them at a subconscious level. We now know that when we endure a great trauma—whether a one-time event or an ongoing experience—we can diminish its negative effects in order to go forward without being held back by emotional scars. That is how powerful the mind is and how resilient the personality. However this does not apply to the personality-disordered individual whose damage is so extensive, that methodologies for repair and recovery do not exist. Negative and positive thinking can exert powerful influences over the conscious mind, but they do not penetrate to the subconscious mind and become programming (or re-programming) unless they are experiential (believed and felt) and until they are consistent with the self image expressed through the personality. For example, a woman with an adequate self image who goes through a negative event can emerge unscathed because her self image is strong enough to protect her. That is, her self image is not consistent with the adverse experience, so it does not "get into" her. But when a woman with an inadequate self image goes through a traumatic event, particularly one of an ongoing nature such as domestic violence, her self image is not strong enough to protect her and it does "get into" her and further degrade her. This principle is key to understanding how and why abusive relationships occur and how to recover from them.

Even though each of us is an individual, with personalities as unique as our DNA and fingerprints, the type of behaviors that unfold in pathological love relationships are not. The personality-disordered person does particular things in a generally predictable way. This means that with some knowledge of this, these individuals become identifiable and these relationships become avoidable. In other words, once the rules of the game are understood, these crimes become predictable. And if they become predictable, they might also become preventable.

As I filtered Donna's experience through what I was learning, I kept coming to the question of "why isn't this taught in school?" I understood why neither of my parents had taught me about it—they didn't know about it because neither of them had grown up in a pathologically dysfunctional family. This was something that existed outside their context. But this subject has been researched and codified for well over 200 years. We were taught in school how to have safe sex, how to avoid obesity and diabetes, how to respond to a bully, but not how to avoid human predators. This is a topic of many layers, so let's get started.

3 A Relationship with a Mask

Finding yourself in a relationship that "turns" is like waking up with a stranger in your bed. You feel confusion, embarrassment, vulnerability and unmistakable menace. Living through it day to day is like being in a maze with a monster. You're frightened all the time, but you know you can't show it. You fumble along trying to keep your wits about you because you know panic could be fatal. You search for reason, safety and understanding, but find none. The farther into the experience you go, the darker and more dire things get and the more lost you become.

Your mind and your heart are at odds. You lie awake at night, your head throbs and your heart pounds. Your mind tells you something is wrong. Your heart tells you to keep on. You loved this man, you vowed to be with him; but what has happened to him, why is he acting this way and what is he going to do next?

You could lie awake at night for the rest of your life and never make sense of it because it makes no sense—until you get the big picture. It is a picture of many things from long ago—of heredity so horrendous or parenting so evil, that it creates a pathology so extreme it affects successive generations. Family violence, whether overt or covert, can do irreparable harm. Abused baby boys grow up to be perpetrators who do more or less what was done to them and/or what they witnessed. Abused baby girls mostly grow up to be victims having become habituated to mistreatment, although a miniscule percent defy their DNA and grow up to be perpetrators. Horse trainers Monty Roberts and Buck Brannaman are examples of this rare outcome. Their fathers beat and brutalized their mothers, their siblings, them and the family horses (in two cases almost to death), but both of them overcame that trauma to not only lead non-violent lives, but to make compassion and empathy the cornerstone of their work.

The perpetrators of interpersonal abuse fall into two broad categories: emotionally disturbed and personality-disordered.

•	The emotionally disturbed are capable of purging their emotional baggage to learn healthy ways of relating IF they want to. Their desire is the fulcrum upon which the future health and happiness of their relationships depend. When someone wants to get better and engages fully in the therapeutic process, chances are good, they will recover. This principle applies to emotional and physical difficulties.

•	The personality-disordered—regardless of what they say—do not have the organic capacity to recover. It's crucial to understand that a man who is mentally ill—no matter how exciting, romantic or "right" he appears to be—is a ticking time bomb. He is not capable of love (or compassion or guilt or shame) because parts of his brain (frontal and/or temporal lobe) do not function normally. He knows how to play the game of romance, but he does not know how to love. Any woman who gets caught in his trap will be harmed.

The Monster

Beast. Brute. Demon. Devil. Evil. Fiend. Lunatic. Maniac. Monster. These are some of the words used by women to describe the nature of the men they fell for who abused them. In each case, this man seemed "too-good-to-be-true" until the relationship turned and he began to unleash hell. These women are describing psychopathic partners.

The psychopath is someone who is organically personality disordered and mentally ill because part of their brain does not function normally. When psychopathy was first studied in the 19th century it was described as "moral insanity" because the behavior of the afflicted was so inhumane and unscrupulous. The top-tier hallmark of this condition presents as "lack of empathy" and the group of characteristics (Cluster B) that manifest in behavior is best described as a "lack of conscience."

In a narrow sense, conscience can be described as the internal mechanism that guides right-and-wrong decisions, perspectives and behaviors, which hopefully result in doing the right thing, even if no one is looking. A compassionate person of conscience stops to help an injured animal instead of driving by, returns a wallet they find on the street, works late to meet a deadline, does what they say they'll do. The implications of persons who do not possess this internal mechanism, who have no sense of right-and-wrong, who have no inner guidance to do the right thing are huge. They hit a pedestrian and keep going, they take money out of a co-worker's desk, they make excuses for not doing their work, they lie and cheat to get what they want.

In some contexts, the psychopath can be distinguished as primary and secondary. They both participate in abuse for personal gratification and personal gain, but at different levels.

• The primary psychopath has a principal role in causing pain and suffering to the victim—he applies the blows, metes out punishment, withholds food, etc.

• The secondary psychopath plays a supporting role—he performs necessary duties to support the primary psychopath, he observes or tolerates the abuse, he condones it by keeping quiet about it.

For example, in dog fighting or human trafficking, the primary psychopath would be the one who abuses the victims for profit, the secondary psychopaths would be the ones who work for him and pay to watch the dog fight or exploit the sex slave. Each psychopath participates at a level that is commensurate to his particular needs.

The Hunt

Women, children, animals, drugs, money and power are the most readily identifiable prey. In every environment that draws a significant number of desirable prey, there will be one or more psychopaths installed where they can get access to the prey, such as:

• gyms, parks and spas
• modeling and acting
• pediatrics and day-care centers
• elementary schools and child services
• animal shelters and research labs
• zoos and training facilities
• pharmacies and hospitals
• college campuses and coffeehouses
• bars, clubs and casinos
• brokerage houses and financial counseling
• business schools and the professions
• capital venture and corporations

- all levels of government

Psychologists say that within the general population, one to four percent is psychopathic; within positions of influence, that percentage rises to six or more. These don't seem like significant numbers until you consider that each psychopath has many victims.

- The charismatic con artist that preys on women may have several dozen to several hundred in his lifetime
- The average pedophile molests or stalks hundreds of children in his lifetime, assaulting or murdering about 130 of them
- The white collar criminal can con thousands, the political tyrant can victimize and destroy millions

Psychopaths are uniquely disposed to conduct cons or frauds because they are masters of deceit and are unimpeded by conscience. They deceive themselves with denial and delusions of grandeur (among other things), they deceive others with charm and pathological lying (among other things). Even though abundant red flags fly over their lives and their relationships, it's impossible to see through their game until you know their secret modus operandi. Their ability to camouflage their true nature and select their victim is chilling, which capabilities factor in their success at manipulating and using others. Besides being hard to detect, they succeed because their behavior is so egregious as to be beyond belief. These men do things to their wives, children and pets so extreme that the uninitiated describe their acts as "unbelievable" and "unconscionable."

Permanent and Progressive

The psychopath's condition is permanent and progressive; their rate of recidivism 100 percent. After the equivalent of a half trillion dollars spent worldwide on research for them, there have yet to be found any therapeutic options. Holland and Canada are just two countries where massive work has been done in recent decades to try to help the psychopath.

• Dutch Ministry of Justice Department Head Jacqueline Hockstenback said, "We know there is no effective treatment for psychopathy."

• After four decades of pioneering research in the Canadian penal system, Robert Hare, PhD said, "Compared to other major clinical disorders... psychopathy ... is responsible for far more social distress and disruption than all other psychiatric disorders combined."

Another important finding of all that research is this: those who receive therapy and treatment do not get better, they simply get more cunning.

The Origins

Violence begets violence—it is the generationally transmitted disease that parents give to their children. With the exception of hereditary transmission, the psychopath is made, not born by:

• trauma in-utero (sensory, chemical, physical)

• trauma in early childhood (family violence, natural disaster, war)

• extreme substance abuse (alcohol, drugs, pharmaceuticals)

• traumatic head injury

Other factors discussed by psychopaths and their victims, that could contribute to the development of psychopathic traits include:

- extreme spoiling
- pornography addiction
- violent media
- occult practices

The psychopath is predatory not passive—he does not sit and wait for prey; he goes out and hunts them. The online predator, the charismatic con artist is aggressive. Whatever his particular hunger, he is always on the prowl to sate it. Even when newly married, the psychopath is always looking for new prey. Many wives have found out after the fact that their husband was not just a player, but an online predator. The exception to this is the older predator whose pathology is so advanced that he has dropped his mask of sanity and is preying at every opportunity. This is a demonstration of the progressive aspect of psychopathy—the derangement intensifies with age and so does their predation. They need more blood, more money, more flesh, more drugs, more power, more thrill and so forth to be temporarily satisfied.

First Signs

Note: one-time acts and mild or transitory manifestations do not indicate brain damage behind a psychopathic personality disorder. Psychopathy expresses in established patterns of extreme behaviors pursued intensively to inflict ever greater harm.

After the brain has developed, the brain-damaged child will begin to reveal his affliction in the elementary and middle school years. As time goes by, whatever predilections begin to emerge will be pursued with more and more intensity. It is during these years that the developing psychopath samples many kinds of abuse and cruelty to find what gives him the most gratification. Once he has fastened upon his predation(s) of choice, he will spend the rest of his life refining his methods of procurement and dispatch.

Early hallmarks include extreme:

- Selfishness (drive for gratification)
- Self-centeredness (narcissism)
- Bullying (financial, physical, verbal)
- Sneaking (to abuse in private to maintain image)
- Perversity (personal habits, sexuality, thinking)
- Promiscuity (experimentation, bestiality)
- Criminality (juvenile delinquency to gang violence)
- Recklessness (financial, physical, sexual, verbal)
- Cruelty to animals (extreme callousness, savagery)
- Mimicry (for purposes of social acceptability)
- Shallowness (mental, emotional, social, sexual)

In the early school years, the developing psychopath displays a lack of natural awareness and genuine interest in anything outside himself. His primary motive is to get his needs met. He may throw tantrums, sulk or withdraw when he doesn't get what he wants, he may wet the bed well into childhood. He may begin to practice manipulating others for his own ends.

In later childhood, he has developed into a bully and a sneak. He chooses targets that are smaller and weaker than him, who have done nothing to provoke him. He frightens and torments them in secret. His targets may be animal and human. If they can't defend themselves or don't fight back, the bullying will gradually escalate until it stopped by the death of the victim or some external circumstance, such as being discovered or interrupted. He doesn't just want to dominate his victims, he wants to hurt them.

In adolescence, the developing psychopath experiments with behaviors that give him a rush: alcohol, cars, crime, drugs, girls. He will experiment with animal torture, sexual sadism or pornography for gratification. He is beginning to understand two things: he is different and he needs to hide his true nature.

Later Signs

As the afflicted leaves childhood and the teen years, he knows what he likes. His predilections are becoming established as habits of mind and behavior. His methods are refined, too and will be more so with every passing year because they are what he lives for.

Although not known to be of high intelligence, the psychopath possesses great predatory cunning. His ability to camouflage his true nature is the little hinge that swings the big door. This is what allows him to move through society undetected whereby he can get access to his prey of choice. His success as a predator depends upon his ability to conceal his deception. The psychopath whose prey of choice is a woman must be able to achieve intimate access in order to run his con.

By early adulthood, the abuser has developed one or more preferred channels for gratification. The 20s are spent refining the procurement of targets, self satisfaction and social acceptability. He knows people but has no close friends. He is involved in activities that provide rush and keep him from having to face himself like drinking, gambling, hunting, racing, burglarizing, carjacking, bronc busting, etc.

In mid-life, the abuser may not only possess advanced tools for trapping victims, but he may have constructed an effective method and have the resources to be quite dangerous to his potential victims.

4 Neuroscience Perspectives

Whether a woman is involved with a low-level abuser, a psychopath or possessed person, the relationship will be structured in a predictable way.

The Pattern

It is called the Cycle of Abuse, the Escalation Cycle, the Wheel of Violence, etc. One of the telltale characteristics of a pathological relationship is this cycle, with its distinct, repeating phases. The end result of each complete cycle delivers more damage to the victim and more power to the abuser. Its dynamics are not easy to identify, even though they are continuously in motion. The escalation cycle is often described as having these main components:

- Increasing Tension
- Explosive Outburst
- Quiet Manipulation

During the Increasing Tension stage, the victim "walks on eggshells" as she seeks to delay or mitigate an outburst. The abuser knows he is in control and taunts his victim. He knows the chances of any challenge or resistance to his provocations are small. The victim tries to protect herself and her dependents (children and animals) by staying out of his way. Denial and withdrawal are other strategies she uses internally and externally to cope with the stress of inevitable, but unpredictable abuse. The Increasing Tension stage can last for days or weeks, even months.

Then comes the Explosive Outburst stage when the abuser gets violent, vents his rage and unleashes his torments. This is when mental, emotional and spiritual abuse intensify; they often, but not always, transmogrify into acts of physical injury, sexual assault, murder, animal abuse, property damage. Sometimes the violence is verbal and mental explicit condemnations and threats. Except in cases where the abuser has caused visible damage, he is unlikely to feel shame or guilt about what he has done. He has asserted his control and put his victim in her place. This is how he lives. The victim has little or no control of outcomes at this time. Women who are wounded during physical attacks sometimes say they don't feel their injuries until much later. They "check out" or "trance out" as a means of coping with the horror. The Explosive Outburst stage is the most violent part of the escalation cycle, but also the briefest, lasting a minute, an hour, perhaps a day.

After energies are spent, the Manipulation stage is set. Even though the psychopathic partner is incapable of emotions like guilt, shame or embarrassment, he has mental awareness of them and knows how and when to "employ" them for his own benefit. His victim may not be able to distinguish his feigned contrition for the real thing the first time or two, but she will eventually learn that it is an act. He may apologize to his victim, even to the point of romancing her and promising never to "lose it" again or he may not say a thing. Either way, it is an uneasy quiet for the victim, a temporary respite. After his outburst, he has soothed the beast, vented his wrath, discharged his tension. The household is allowed to return to "normal" and things are quiet for while. This is a time of increased vulnerability for the victim; this is when she may find herself succumbing to emotions described as Stockholm Syndrome in an effort to survive. The abuser will later reveal that he uses the time in-between his explosive outbursts to justify a previous event or set up a future event. The Quiet Manipulation stage can be the longest part of the cycle.

Most of the descriptions of the repetitive phases of an abusive relationship express its intrusiveness, imbalance of power, inequality of rights, diversity of abuse forms and social tolerance of mistreatment. It is personally and socially valuable to grasp the operative principles so that they can be recognized, avoided and where possible, remedied.

Normalcy Bias

A common reaction to an encounter with the unreality that only the dangerously deranged can arrange (emphasis on the concept of unreality) is normalcy bias. For millions, it is an incapacitating response to abuse. It is a natural, but uninformed reaction to a misunderstood or unrecognized risk that leads to disaster. It's like trying to run from a grizzly bear, steer out of a skid or get sympathy from the devil. It's an all-but impossible situation that often leads to a violent end.

Over time, normalcy bias depletes and incapacitates because it is a reaction to the worst kind of stress there is: unrelenting (which also happens to be a characteristic of psychopathic abuse). Normalcy bias can be described as inaccurate, inadequate thinking that makes things worse. It occurs in the most dire circumstances as a freeze or panic response.

The freeze response is withering; it shows up as the too-little-too-late of timidity or the never-even-trying of immobility. Caution and circumspection serve, immobility and timidity prohibit. Immobility is not just never leaping, it's never looking. The immobilized watch the world go by; they lead a "sort of" life. Some become armchair critics, some become bitter, some become dull.

The psychological run-up to normalcy bias is this: the person thinks that since something has never happened before, it never will. It is one of the ravages of abuse you can see–if you know what to look for–in the countenance of someone who is being abused. Normalcy bias can show up like this in language:

- "Oh, he would never hurt me."
- "I leave my kids with her all the time."
- "His first wife just didn't understand him."
- "She's not after my money."

Abusive relationships are counterfeit and counter-intuitive experiences. They're counterfeit in that they start out like romance but turn into assault. They're counter-intuitive in that what works in a healthy relationship does not bear fruit in an unhealthy one. Normalcy bias comes from not knowing what you're dealing with. To make matters more confusing, normalcy bias can manifest as both a cause and a result. As a cause factor, normalcy bias means you do not see the red flags and do not grasp the gravity of the situation, which can work in you like denial. This is one reason bad things happen to good people: they're uninformed (gullibility, naiveté) and therefore unprepared for the unthinkable.

When you're faced with a situation you've ever experienced, the typical reaction is to downplay/forgive/overlook its seriousness and go along in expectation of a nothing-out-of-the-ordinary result. In the world of pathological relationships (personal or professional), this kind of thinking can and does lead to ruin.

Denial and naiveté, real or postured, may delay the onslaught, but they will not save you from the ravages of an abusive individual (or organization). In fact, this frame of mind actually makes you more vulnerable. Denial does not change reality. Naiveté does not change reality. Just because you cannot imagine or refuse to accept something doesn't mean it doesn't exist. This kind of mindset sets you up to be less able to deal with the extreme circumstances that are heading your way.

After just two months of marriage, the wife realizes that all three of her animals have been harmed in the same time frame. The cat appeared with a broken leg, the dog became violently ill after ingesting something poisonous and the parrot started dropping feathers. She tells herself it's coincidental. She knows her husband knows she loves her animals. In the extra-full days of being a newlywed, she doesn't notice that her cat has become nervous, her dog defensive and both have had multiple accidents indoors despite being previously perfectly housetrained for years. Six months later, the cat has disappeared, the dog has been euthanized after being hit by a car when the wife wasn't home and the parrot has died in her cage of unexplained causes.

When you face a situation you've never imagined, it's not uncommon to downplay the risks and go along in hopes of nothing out of the ordinary happening. However, when a worst-case scenario unfolds, you become prone to over- or under-react in order to escape pain and return to normalcy. Many times, that's as useful as wishful thinking.

In an abusive relationship, an over-reaction can lead to violent reprisal, an under-reaction can lead to abject submission; either of which can be life-changing or life-ending.

As a result factor, normalcy bias sets in when you are beginning to break down under the strain of unrelenting stress. This is the kind of stress that kills. It depletes body, mind and spirit. It impairs thinking, dulls feelings and shuts down life force. This is the experience that leads to the post-traumatic stress disorder (PTSD) suffered by veterans of war and veterans of relationship violence.

Normalcy bias accelerates when you're weak and getting weaker; it exacerbates the crumbling of your faculties. As a result, you make poorer and poorer decisions. And as you do, the consequences become more and more grave, which effects lead to added, unnecessary suffering and death.

During a day-long hike in the back country, the wife becomes aware that her husband is getting farther and farther ahead of her. He is in great shape and he is familiar with the territory; she is neither. She doesn't want to hold him back, so she doesn't ask him to slow down. She climbs and hikes as fast as she can. Within half an hour, he is out of range and she is, for all practical purposes, alone. As anxiety wraps its cold fingers around her, she scolds herself for letting it happen. She imagines a mountain lion behind every boulder and a grizzly bear in each stand of trees. Her husband has the flashlight, ponchos, bear spray and water bottle. She comes to a fork in the trail and cannot see his foot prints. She does not know which way to go.

She screams and waits for a response that doesn't come. Unable to contain her panic, she begins to run and eventually trips over a tree root. She falls hard, splitting her lip, breaking her wrist and spraining her ankle. Shivering in the coming cold of a mountain night, she crawls to a fir tree and gets up under its skirt. It is late in the tourist season and it could be weeks before anyone comes this way. And it is.

Normalcy bias is an important but little known factor of the extreme mental, emotional and spiritual exhaustion of being trapped in a pathological situation.
Millions of people waste their lives in hopelessly abusive relationships because they simply do not realize their partner is incapable of love.

The Neuroscience the Mask Hides

Neuroscience has made great strides in recent years, including how to apply it to people on both sides of the equation of an abusive relationship, which by the way, could be represented like this:

NEED TO CONTROL + INADEQUATE SELF IMAGE = ABUSE

What has been discovered about the human brain in recent years has great bearing on prospects (or lack of) for the abuser and the abused. From the latest research in neuroscience, we now know that the brain:
•   Works as a full-time, unemotional, goal-seeking mechanism
•   Subconsciously seeks to replicate or substantiate whatever it has been "fed" and accepted as reality, whether the input was true or false

- Is unable to distinguish between actual experience and virtual experience
- Is capable of making and breaking synapses (the physiological basis of mental habits) based on repetitious input (neuroplasticity)

In other words, the brain is highly programmable. This is how and why brainwashing works—and this is how and why women get programmed by abuse and succumb to its meta messages. Psychologists say that the universal would is "I'm not good enough." For millions of women, the meta message of abuse is like salt in the wound, "I'm nothing, I don't matter, I have no value." Over time, these cruel and untrue messages go deep into the subconscious and become part of your programming for life. If unchallenged and unchecked, they can do more damage to self image and in some cases, the will to live. The good news is that neuroplasticity works both ways—when you want to, you can bounce back.

Once you take note of a problem, your brain starts working toward the solution. The first step is taking note.

The Organic Nature of Psychopathy

The organic brain damage characterized as psychopathy is permanent and progressive. Every normal person would benefit from understanding the magnitude of this and would be wise to give it due thought because psychopathy affects them, whether they realize it or not. Psychopathic behaviors differ between intimate relationships and organizational ones because of context and scale, but their goal is the same: to control and destroy.

When you look around and see that many things are getting worse, does it occur to you that psychopathy could be playing a role in it or do you think it's just the ebb and flow of a relationship, a company, a civilization? Taken together, the proclivities of the psychopath eventually destroy. The destructions they visit on their prey express incomprehensible cruelty and waste. Most of us have never recognized these things to a great degree. This could change. In considering the fate of formerly great organizations and societies around the world, the fingerprints of psychopaths are all over their economic, moral and social decay. The insanity of the psychopath expresses itself in many ways, but its common denominator is annihilation.

5 Psychological Perspectives

In the last two centuries, the personality-disordered have been called insane without delirium, morally insane and most recently, psychopathic. Though the names have changed, their reality has not; they are *other*.

Psychopaths and the possessed want you to think they look like monsters, when in reality, most of them look normal, even appealing. There is nothing about their appearance that gives them away—until they reach a point in adulthood (which varies by individual) when their pathology has grown beyond their ability to manage it. It becomes too intense for them to camouflage. Because it is progressive there comes a time when the mask begins to crack and public conduct begins to reveal their true nature. This is a small respite for society—the sickest of the psychopathic tend to go too far and expose themselves. By the time the mask cracks however, the abuse he has been dishing out behind closed doors has been prolonged and pronounced; his victim(s) may already be damaged or dead.

Although the social predator lives to achieve control over others, he has little control over himself. He denies, justifies and minimizes his abuse of his abuse of his victim by saying that sometimes he "just loses control of himself" when what he is really doing is creating or manipulating circumstances to seize more control of her. This critical distinction is well put by Lundy Bancroft who has three decades of experience working with abusive men in anger management programs. In WHY

DOES HE DO THAT? Bancroft opens the door into the mind of the controlling and abusive male:

"An abusive man often considers it his right to control where his partner goes, with whom she associates, what she wears, and when she needs to be back home. He therefore feels that she should be grateful for any freedoms he does grant her…"

Thanks to the work of Drs. Hervey Cleckley, Robert Hare and those who preceded them, we have a reliable basis for identifying and assessing of the attributes of the psychopath. Although much of this work was created for those in the helping professions, it provides a reliable guide for learning how to recognize the real and present danger of the psychopath. A good place to begin is to know the origins of the brain damage that causes psychopathy:

- genetics
- early childhood trauma
- head injury
- substance abuse
- pharmaceuticals
- demonic possession

Babies who are born with a genetic predisposition to psychopathy grow into it. By early childhood, there can be the first signs. Toddlers damaged by violence in the home begin to exhibit marked self-centeredness and anti-social intentions—callousness and cruelty is often the first sign of a child who does not have a conscience. Individuals who sustain severe head injuries, substance abuse (to include pharmaceuticals) begin to show signs of altered behavior and thinking after their physical or chemical trauma—extreme mood swings and erratic thinking are first signs of induced psychopathy. Interestingly, a priest who worked with doctors and psychiatrists for many decades in Europe, the Middle East and the US, observed that half of the psychiatric patients he examined were not psychopathic, but demon possessed. Further, he reported that all of his cases were successfully resolved through exorcism.

When you know what to look for, you can learn to see the psychopath well in advance of his own behavior blowing his cover. But until that time, his ability to move undetected through a community or a company makes his job of social predation much easier. Uninformed, unsuspecting prey is much easier to haul down.

When he is on the prowl, which is most of the time, he operates with a persona that appears normal, charming, even magnetic. But what the discerning will observe over time is that while the psychopath is gregarious and outgoing, he has no friends, just acquaintances. This reveals something he cannot hide for long—his incapacity for authentic relationship. He may be a serial womanizer, with dozens of women going through the meat grinder of his charismatic con year after year, but he cannot love.

The psychopath is at the top of the list in the ranks of the most violent and dangerous intimate partner abuse cases. His organic brain damage renders him without the internal brakes of a conscience which, combined with his insatiable drive for gratification, lets him perpetrate heinous abuses on those closest to him. Interpersonal terrorist would not be too strong a term for this type of social predator. Most often, his wife or girlfriend bears the brunt of his savagery, but in 71 percent of these households, children and animals are also tortured and murdered.

In PSYCHOPATHS AMONG US, Dr. Hare wrote:

"Lying is like breathing to the psychopath. When caught in a lie and challenged, they make up new lies, and don't care if they're found out... Lying, deceiving and manipulation are innate talents for psychopaths...When caught in a lie or challenged with the truth, they are seldom perplexed or embarrassed—they simply change their stories or attempt to rework the facts so that they appear to be consistent with the lie. The results are a series of contradictory statements and a thoroughly confused listener. They exhibit a cluster of distinctive personality traits, the most significant of which is an utter lack of conscience. They also have huge egos, short tempers and an appetite for excitement—a dangerous mix...

Dr. Hare (hare.org) has studied them in prison and taught at the university level for four decades. He developed the diagnostic standard that is used today (for clinical, organizational and domestic violence cases) to establish the degree of psychopathic traits present in a perpetrator and whether or not they add up to a diagnosis of full psychopathy.

Note: An individual can possess several traits to a high degree without that leading to a diagnosis of psychopathy. It takes a preponderance of these traits expressed to an extreme degree to warrant a clinical diagnosis. A person who is charming is not psychopathic unless there is a pronounced history of their using that charm to deceive and damage others in the extreme.

In WITHOUT CONSCIENCE, Dr. Hare writes:

"I heard from various psychologists...that the most powerful madness of all when it comes to shaping society is psychopathy... The psychopathic personality can also be very convincing. They may ramble and tell stories that seem unlikely in light of what is known about them... Psychopaths may apologize or show remorse only to get away with something, but in the end you will be stabbed in the back and realize how very shallow their words were. Everyone who knows a psychopath will be stabbed in the back, sooner or later."

The Soulless

When there is no conscience or soul, the highest and best emotions are inaccessible. Love, compassion, tenderness, loyalty, bravery, altruism, sacrifice—all of these are unavailable to the morally insane. Also impossible for the psychopathic is any act of artistic creativity. Ironically, some install themselves in positions in the arts where they pose as creatives by mimicking social behavior and even producing their own output, which tends to be bizarre and/or hideous. One of the distinctions between the sane and the insane is access to higher emotions; this distinction is not hard to see when you know to look for it, but it takes practice to discern the feigned emotions expressed through the pleasing personality of the psychopath (persona) from his real feelings expressed through his true nature (predator). In personal relationships, this dichotomy expresses the counterfeit nature of a psychopathic bond. It also explains more of what women experience when they are being abused by a partner who is incapable of higher emotions. In the public arena, this dichotomy expresses the age-old struggle between good and evil.

Assessing Evil

The public was introduced to forensic psychiatrist Dr. Michael Stone in 2006 when the show based on his work, "Most Evil" debuted on the Discovery Channel. The show profiled murderers (mass and serial) and explored the nature of human evil which he equated to the psychopath.

Michael Stone, M.D. is a professor of Clinical Psychiatry at the College of Physicians and Surgeons at Columbia University and an attending physician in Forensic Psychiatry at Creedmoor Psychiatric Center in New York. At the Mid-Hudson Psychiatric Center in New York he undertook an in-depth study of the biographies of 500 murderers from case files. His purpose was two-fold: to determine why these killers did what they did and to identify the underlying traits that facilitated their violence. From this, he formulated a list of interpretations he called the "22 Levels of Evil" (similar to the circles of Hell in Dante's "The Divine Comedy").

In explaining his list, Dr. Stone said that the first classification is not evil but self defense; he used it as a starting point from which to base the descending trajectory to evil. (Quotations are Dr. Stone's words.)

Level 1: "Those who kill in self defense and do not show psychopathic tendencies."

Dr. Stone describes the second through eighth classifications as impulse crimes arising out of overwhelming emotion and poor impulse control. These behaviors are non-premeditated and reactive. They could be described as crimes of passion, which are typically committed when someone finds himself in an intense and unrestrained situation. Perpetrators of these crimes often feel remorse, such as the jealous lover (Level 2) and the traumatized person who kills in desperation, such as an abused child or battered wife (Level 6).

Level 2: "Jealous lovers who, though egocentric or immature, are not psychopathic; crime of passion."

Level 3: "Willing companions of killers: aberrant personality; probably impulse-ridden, with some anti-social traits."

Level 4: "Those who kill in self-defense, after extremely provocative behavior toward the victim."

Level 5: "Highly narcissistic, but not distinctly psychopathic persons, with a psychotic core, who kill loved ones or family members out of jealousy."

Level 6: "Traumatized, desperate people who kill abusive relatives and others (such as to escape abuse) but lack significant traits. Genuinely remorseful."

Level 7: "Impetuous, hot-headed murderers without psychopathic features."

Level 8: "Highly narcissistic, but not distinctly psychopathic people."

Levels nine through 16 classify acts of rage and ruthlessness, only some of which require low-level psychopathic traits. These killers got into situations using their superficial charm, pathological lying, grandiosity, delusions of grandeur, extreme manipulativeness, then acted out their callousness and remorselessness through murder. On the periphery of this group are murderers whose crimes escalate from surveillance and stalking activities. Dr. Stone describes these as "... people who are hungry for attachment but who know no bounds. There's no brake system preventing them from bothering, pestering and sometimes even harming the object of their interest." This corresponds to lower levels of self control ("braking") observable in youth. Perpetrators who commit this level of violence do not hesitate to murder someone they feel is "in the way" (Level 11) or kill because they want to (Level 15).

Level 9: "Non-psychopathic people with smoldering rage who kill when that rage is ignited."

Level 10: "Jealous lovers with marked psychopathic features."

Level 11: "Killers of people who were in the way (such as witnesses), egocentric, but not distinctly psychopathic."

Level 12: "Power-hungry psychopaths who kill when cornered."

Level 13: "Murderers with inadequate, rage-filled personalities and psychopathic features with a psychotic core, who kill those close to them. Jealously is an underlying motive."

Level 14: "Ruthlessly self-centered psychopathic schemers"

Level 15: "Psychopathic or cold-blooded spree-killers who have committed multiple murders."

Level 16: "Psychopaths committing multiple vicious acts."

The final six levels of evil express full-blown psychopathy in extreme acts of premeditated cruelty and inhumane behavior. The psychopath is driven by an insatiable quest for gratification. When he possesses a majority of deeply entrenched anti-social traits, the result is someone who thrives on delivering pain and watching others suffer. These are the incomprehensible and unimaginable crimes that make the news. These are crimes that often end up in the news.

Dr. Stone identifies children who develop "with no sense of empathy or compassion for others" as "callous-unemotional youths." These are children who develop into psychopaths in adulthood and commit this level of crime. Perpetrators of this type take their time with their victims. They possess an unnerving calm as they commit their acts of perversion, murder and torture (Level 17). It is not uncommon for them to make their crimes into rituals that go on for hours or days because torture is the source of their greatest gratification (Level 22).

As this information demonstrates, psychopaths, although capable of role-playing, are incapable of relationship. Their sex life consists of rape and one-night stands. Many of their crimes, which originate out of their lack of conscience and self control, are likewise done on the fly. They inflict extreme suffering on their victims and then they murder them. They derive more pleasure from the torture than from the murder. When their victims plead for their lives, the psychopath only feels more contempt. The extent to which they are enlivened by extreme psychological and physical anguish is the measure of their sickness.

Level 17: "Sexually perverse serial murderers and/or torture-murderers. Murder is the primary motive, following prolonged torture (among males rape is the primary motive, with murder to hide the evidence), systematic torture is not a primary factor".

Level 18: "Torture murderers with murder the primary motive."

Level 19: "Psychopaths driven to terrorism, subjugation, intimidation and rape, but short of murder."

Level 20: "Torture murderers with torture as the primary motive but in psychopathic personalities."

Level 21: "Psychopaths preoccupied with torture in the extreme, but not known to have committed murder."

Level 22: "Psychopathic, serial torture-murderers, with torture the primary motive."

Dr. Stone relates that about 90 percent of serial murderers can be classified as psychopaths. He believes that more than half of these were damaged as young children by the failure of their parents to love and protect them. The stress this caused them altered their brain chemistry to the point that the frontal and sometimes the temporal lobe(s) did not develop properly.
As a result, they wander the earth alone, incapable of creativity and love (because they do not have access to any of the higher emotions) and act out their primal wounds by abusing others. Early exposure and

subsequent addictions to alcohol, drugs, pornography and video violence can also figure in the formation of the human evil that is the psychopath.

Dr. Stone summarized what he saw in the minds of serial killers this way:

"... more than 90 percent meet criteria, hard criteria for psychopathy. Almost all of them are sadists... where there's enjoyment of the suffering of others as a key quality, and a love of control and domination of others, etc. Half of them are loners, men that can't make long relationships with others. So in effect, some of them use serial killing as a way of having a one-night stand where they rape the woman and then kill her to destroy evidence... Some of them seek revenge... so they're constantly getting back at the parents who abused them or neglected them...And another motive... killing a specific parent over and over, but not actually killing the parent... terrible, terrible childhoods... So the bulk of them; however, have come from horrible homes where the early damage and misery becomes a motivating force later for seeking revenge... they don't have the social skills to compensate for that and to make a good relationship anyway and kind of get past it. So they're stuck, they're mired in the misery of their childhood forever."

Dr. Stone's work does not explore other realms of evil such as the white-collar criminal. This type of psychopath operates in a position of influence that allows him access to his preferred prey and form of gratification. Most of these organizational psychopaths do not commit murder, but their actions can lead to large-scale suffering of all kinds, including death.

SNAKES IN SUITS, WHEN PSYCHOPATHS GO TO WORK by Paul Babiak, PhD and Robert Hare, PhD delves into evil in high places. The 2012 film, "Fishead" depicts the world of the organizational psychopath through interviews with leading thinkers from diverse vantage points. Both provide valuable introductions into what happens in an organization, to which certain predators are drawn, when the psychopath gets into an office or position of power. Almost all of the abuse is perpetrated out of sight. None is so diabolical as that of the human being who has been taken over by spiritual evil.

6 Biblical Perspectives

When they are being abused, one of the first questions many women ask is, "What is wrong with me that I have attracted this sick man into my life?"

Asking this question evidences the emotional depth to take responsibility and the mental maturity to face the fact that a dreamy relationship that has turned into a nightmarish prison. This is a willingness that wants to address the problem, (which her partner has told her is all her fault) so that the relationship can go back to "normal" and get better.

The willingness to be accountable for one's own actions is crucial to having healthy relationships and living an honest life. This willingness is not present in the mind of the most toxic partners, although they may act as if it is, because they are psychopathic or possessed.

In the context of relationships that "turn" I have found that the journey to knowledge and the process of healing requires more than can be found within the confines of psychology. Man's organization of human behavior is where many of us turn when we come face-to-face with something that is bigger than us and defies our current understanding.

Psychology is where Donna and our family first turned when our own understanding proved inadequate to the situation. Two years later, I happened to find an interview that shed a whole new light on things by exposing links between pathological behavior and demonic possession.

Merriam Webster defines the demonic as "an evil spirit, a source or agent of evil, harm, distress or ruin." It could also be said that the demonic works in opposition to that which is of God. Keep in mind that, like the predator in the human equation of a predator/prey relationship, demons also seek those whose attributes give them an opening.

Before man monetized the legal system and came up with the psychological disciplines, dangerous people were considered possessed and treated accordingly—they were taken out of society—they were typically killed in order to remove their evil from the community. I found a series of interviews with a Jesuit priest and diplomat who participated in thousands exorcisms during his lifetime and later wrote about them. In his books, Father Malachi Martin shared his fantastic experiences of doing battle with evil:

"Like a mongoose playing a cobra, the priest will attempt to work the demon into a position first of disadvantage, then of vulnerability. He begins by demanding, with the authority of prayer, to know its name. The demons are not always willing to play this game. They lie silent, sullen and hidden. When this happens, the exorcist must provoke them into breaking cover. You have to tease them out."

According to Father Martin, there are different types of possession, with "perfect possession" being the worst type, the state in which a person has lost complete control and is at the mercy of spiritual evil.

From his half century of direct experience, his observations about demonic interference in human existence are these:

•   There is a difference between spiritual oppression and demonic possession

- Over a 50-year period in his lifetime, there was a staggering increase in acts of evil in general and an 800 percent increase in documented cases of possession
- Half of psychiatric patients diagnosed as psychotic were not insane, but were possessed and recovered completely when treated as such
- Exorcisms were only performed at the request of the possessed and/or the family
- Exorcisms did not go forward until the possessed passed a medical and psychiatric evaluation
- At least one medical doctor was present at every exorcism and often, a psychiatrist was present, too
- The possessed were all found to have done something that created an opening for evil to enter them
- Playing with a Ouija board was found to be one of the most common conduits for demonic entry
- Channeling and illicit sex were other activities that opened the participant(s) to demonic influences
- Other forms of dabbling in occult practices were found to be just as dangerous in terms of exposure to spiritual evil
- The purpose of evil and the goal of a demon is to destroy the body and soul of the possessed
- Nominal ("lukewarm") Christians are their preferred prey
- The dominant energy of the demonic is hatred so extreme it cannot be adequately stated with language
- More than one psychiatrist left his profession after witnessing a single exorcism
- Many atheists converted to Christianity after witnessing a single exorcism
- Many participants in exorcism died in the months following the ritual

- Exorcisms could last a few hours or go on for several months
- The exorcised spirits are not destroyed, they are simply evicted from the possessed
- Demonic spirits are all around us at all times
- Cases of perfect possession are beyond the scope of exorcism, there is no deliverance for them

Father Martin describes the battle with demons this way:

"The demon does not physically inhabit the body; it possesses the person's will. We have to compel the thing to reveal itself and its purpose. It can be slow and difficult, with the demon taunting, scorning, abusing you–speaking through the mouth of the possessed, but not in his or her voice... In the end, though, it does come out – and when that happens you experience the sensation we call 'presence'. At that moment you know you are in the company of the purest evil. I have felt the claws of invisible animals tearing at my face. I have been knocked off my feet, blinded and winded. But it is then, when you've sensed the 'presence' that the real attack on the demon can begin...

"The whole nature of the thing changes. The demon knows it's losing. Instead of screaming abuse, it begins to plead for mercy. It says it's sorry, it begs to be spared. It promises to go home...

"Where they go, I do not know. We do not destroy them, we drive them out. Sometime I encounter the same ones again. As the demon disappears, the person it has possessed is 'cleared' and a wondrous wave of peace comes over them."

The following themes are found in the Bible about the relationship between mental and physical illness and demonic activity:

•   When it is in the body, it develops as a result of inherent sin nature. It can cause additional problems that affect physical health.

•   When it is in the will (mind and heart), it develops as a result of giving in to baser nature. Corrupted behavior can lead to corrupted thoughts and put the afflicted person into a closed loop of suffering.

•   When it is in the spirit, it comes as a result of direct attack by a demon or influence by a demonic spirit.

•   A person without much knowledge of and faith in God is open to demonic possession and in fact, is its most preferred prey.

•   A person who is firm in their faith, even if it is new, is not subject to possession, however, he or she can be oppressed by demonic spirits or by a demon itself.

All demonic activity can lead to additional problems. Each cause of mental illness responds to or requires a particular treatment for healing to occur:

•   Neurological disturbances, such as brain dysfunction, respond to physical treatment.

•   Psychological disorders require confession, counseling and the implementation of higher principles of conduct.

•   Supernatural disturbances, such as demon possession, require massive spiritual intervention and the use of Christ's name.

Oppression and Possession

Oppression and possession are two distinct categories of demonic activity, which differ in nature and degree. Both can afflict the victim in multiple ways and both can be caused by more than one spirit.

In the 2000 Bulletin of the World Health Organization, Director General, Dr. G. H. Brundtland listed major depression, schizophrenia, bipolar disorders, alcohol abuse and obsessive-compulsive disorders as the most serious mental health illnesses. The Bible says these disorders can be caused and relieved through spiritual means.

Demonic oppression refers to having demons and spirits acting in opposition to you. To be vexed means to be harassed, tormented or troubled. Demonic oppression most often manifests as "work of the flesh" which sacred texts specify to be:

Adultery   Emulations   Fornication
Wrath Uncleanness   Strife
Lasciviousness   Seditions   Idolatry
Heresies   Witchcraft   Envyings
Hatred Murders   Variance
Revelings   Drunkenness

"Now the works of the flesh are manifest... as I have also told you in time past, that they which do such things shall not inherit the kingdom of God."

Symptoms of Spiritual Oppression

The afflicted is more cognizant of demonic oppression than those around him. He tries to hide the symptoms. When he can't hide them, he makes up reasons for them to deflect blame or responsibility from him, and to deny or minimize consequences for others.

Note: This behavior is congruent with how psychopaths handle their "slip ups".

- Anxiety and fear that is irrational, unusual and intense
- Lapses in rational thinking and acceptable behavior
- Extreme emptiness, loneliness and feelings of loss
- Uncharacteristic conflicts and emotional outbursts
- Unprecedented lack of self control (verbal expression, substance use)
- Loss of direction and interest, aimlessness
- Inability to discern things spiritually
- Overwhelming desire for control, power, material possessions
- Loss of connection to God, lack of fear of God

Causes of Spiritual Oppression

Demonic oppression (like a charismatic con) is predatory and opportunistic. In the latter case, and all it takes is a single, casual contact with something or someone demonic to unleash hell:

- Emotional dishonesty to self and others
- Hedonism to the point of immorality
- Sexual congress with the oppressed or possessed
- Looking at pornography
- Over use of mind-altering substances
- Trying out or joining false religions
- Exploring the occult, directly or indirectly
- Playing with psychic phenomena

- Having or acquiring possessed objects
- Venting rage or wrath on strangers
- Developing extreme jealousy in relationship
- Accepting violence that is unjust (video games)
- Going without sleep or sleeping very little
- Being angry at God

Symptoms of Demonic Possession

The goal of a demon or spiritual evil is to destroy (kill) the afflicted by his own hand or through the rigor of the possession. If others can be destroyed, they will be. It is reported that some possessions last for years without dramatic events; however, when help is sought to expel the demon, the battle becomes pitched.

Note: The last four symptoms in the following list are held to be the most conclusive evidence of true demonic possession by spiritual authorities.

- hyper-sensitivity to light, sound, touch
- lack of interest in food
- intense loneliness with desire to be alone
- personal and social recklessness (appearance and conduct)
- uncontrollable verbal rages with extreme profanity
- speaking in foreign languages unknown to the afflicted (including ancient ones no longer in use)
- refusal to submit to any human or spiritual authority other than the occupying demon(s)
- mental insensibility that renders the person unable to grasp simple spiritual concepts (keeping God at bay)
- display of occult knowledge (necromancy, astral projection)

- utter inattention to physical appearance and wellbeing
- complete lack of restraint (urination, masturbation, sexual advances)
- attempting or wanting to commit suicide
- display of superhuman abilities (levitation, psychokinesis, strength)
- expression of multiple and distinct personalities
- threatening and terrifying behavior (heights, fire, weapons, temperature, animals, objects)
- violent reaction to Christ's name or mention of His crucifixion

Causes of Demonic Possession

Demonic possession happens by exposure to someone or something that is associated with the demonic. Most cases of possession result in the death of the possessed after prolonged suffering.

Note: This corresponds to Levels 20, 21 and 22 of Dr. Stone's Scale of Evil and the highest scores on Dr. Hare's Psychopathy Checklist.

- experimenting with or leading a grossly immoral lifestyle
- having or using occult objects
- seeking or using occult abilities
- giving occult practitioners spiritual access (fortune telling, astrology, psychic reading)
- overtly or covertly rebelling against biblical authority
- blaspheming the Holy Spirit
- spiritual immaturity that includes disrespect of God

7 Barry and Marcia

Marcia was a year shy of vesting her pension with FedEx when she met Barry on the last delivery of her day. She drove down the long drive to the farmhouse and thought how lucky the owners were to live in such an idyllic place. After several more deliveries over the next few months, Barry began to walk out to meet the truck and save her the time of running to the house. One day, he walked up with a pretty mare in hand and her young colt trotting alongside. "He's the same color as your hair."

He said it with a softness that took her back, like they'd known each other for years. He handled the mare with aplomb and Marcia could see from how relaxed both horses were that he knew what he was doing. Like her, he owned Belgians. She left that day feeling just impressed, but moved. She thought about Barry and his farm the rest of the day.

By early summer, the inevitable had happened: Barry had asked her out. They had a nice dinner made all the more enjoyable by his casual, but impeccable manners. He hardly took his eyes off her the entire evening, which felt alternately discomfiting and delicious. By the end of the fourth date, Marcia realized how utterly safe and comfortable she felt with this man. He asked if she'd like to stop by his barn to see a late-season colt that had been born the previous week. She said yes. They spent a half hour watching the newborn with his dam and talking together easily. As they walked out of the barn, he hugged her shoulders and lightly kissed the side of her head. She felt his lips through her hair and nearly gasped. She wanted him to kiss her again, but he didn't. He opened the truck door for her and drove her home. The summer went by in a blink. More dates, more time with horses, more kisses, more conversation, more knowing looks. For the first time in her life, Marcia felt completely accepted and wanted. In their hurried encounters when she was making deliveries and their unrushed reveries on weekends, she slowly opened her heart to this man's kindred spirit, pouring out her deepest wounds and fondest wishes.

In the midst of all this, something happened to the first colt Marcia had met and he died. The vet said he died of dehydration, but Barry said that didn't make sense because he was with his mother and she was fine. Marcia stood witness as Barry dug a hole with the backhoe and put the beautiful young horse to rest.

He was a third-generation horseman. He'd inherited the family homestead with all of its equipment and some of his horses when an injury retired his dad from full-time duties. His parents lived in a house farther back on the property. Barry made a good living growing hay and logging trees in the woods with his draft horses. For fun, he'd started entering pulling competitions at the local level and quickly moved up through the ranks. Marcia was also working with her horses and entering them in some shows, but without as much ease or success on account of her work schedule. She had a pair of powerful young geldings who were doing well that she wanted to campaign.

When Barry asked her to move in with him on Labor Day weekend, she said "yes." When he proposed two weeks later, she blinked back tears and said "yes." When he suggested they elope, she shook her head, but he talked her into it and elope they did the very next week. She really had to wrangle for time off on such short notice, but she did.

The first month of marriage was a continuation and enlargement of everything that had gone before it. Every day was a gift. Marcia felt like she floated on air and reveled in the amazing turn her life had taken in the space of a few months. Barry made her feel welcome in his home; he made room for her horses. He helped her make dinner and they talked about everything.

A couple of her horses got banged up by his, but it was nothing serious and she knew horses would be horses. One evening she looked out and saw one of her horses limping badly. She ran out, lifted up his enormous hoof and was stunned to see a huge nail going straight up through it. She had to cut away part of the inner hoof to get purchase on the nail and pull it out. The horse was lame for three weeks, partially due to the size of the nail hole and partially due to infection. She was relieved they had been spared tetanus.

The second month, she got four flat tires driving to work. When she called Barry for help, she got his voicemail, which meant he was outside without his cell phone—again. He was apologetic when she told him about the flat and her unanswered calls. He promised he would keep his cell phone on him. She didn't get any more flat tires after that.

The next month, her other horse must have run into something because she came home to find him with a three foot laceration running from his shoulder to his flank. It wasn't deep, but it was ugly. This required a vet call and more follow-up care than the hoof injury. The vet said it looked like a blade cut because it was so clean. Marcia couldn't imagine what was in the pasture that the horse had moved against. She scoured every square of the barns and pastures without finding anything. She was mystified. None of Barry's horses had ever picked up a nail or cut themselves the way hers had. This injury was going to leave a long scar, like a seam.

Barry kept an eye on the horses while Marcia was at work and doctored their wounds, but they weren't healing easily or well. They were also becoming nervous and difficult to handle--something they had never been. As the weather cooled, Marcia felt weary with the growing burdens of her job, her marriage and her horses. Just as quickly as her luck had changed and she'd met and married Barry, now it seemed she was under a ban. Nothing was working out and everything seemed to be so time-consuming. She was so distracted, she started misplacing things. She'd spend frantic minutes every day searching for her keys, her wallet, her cell phone, her contacts, etc. She wondered why she was doing this all of a sudden. One Saturday afternoon, she was in the tack room looking for a headstall she knew she'd cleaned and hung up, but it was not there. She was fed up. Barry walked just as she was about to throw a buckle in frustration. He looked at her and laughed in a way she hadn't heard in weeks. It melted her heart and she laughed, too. "I think you are working way too hard." He wrapped his arms around her and she leaned into his bulk. His flannel shirt smelled like man and horse. She felt the visceral sense of his understanding for the first time in many weeks and it made her weak in the knees. How could she lose touch with how much he "got" her?

It was one of the many gifts he'd given her and yet she'd let it slip in the drain of daily living.

The next morning it rained. They sat in the sun room and looked out over the farm drinking their coffee. "Why don't you quit work, stay at home and do what you want to do?"

The thought had never crossed her mind. Rather, she hadn't dared to consider such a thing. She just looked at him, speechless. That evening, he turned out the light and they lay there in the dark. "If you want to, you can, you know."

She closed her eyes, but didn't sleep. She chewed on the idea for weeks. She was six months away from vesting. She didn't dare quit before then--that would be too scary. Every few days, Barry encouraged her without pressure to think about the difference between continuing to run in the hamster wheel versus being home with him and the horses full time. He didn't need to tell her what it would mean to their hopes of campaigning their horses. She felt inadequate in so many ways as she thought about the net effect of being pulled in so many directions. Once she'd married Barry, she had all but lost interest in her career. She was appalled at what it had meant to her before, when she'd needed it. She was a hamster running a wheel, and her was an opportunity to get off the wheel and out of the cage. But if she stuck it out 25 more weeks, she'd have her pension. She told Barry that's what she was going to do. She could stand it for 22 more weeks. He shrugged and nodded. "Whatever you want."

He didn't say he was disappointed, but she could tell. The next week, the steering went out in her truck on the way to work and she careened off the road. She hit a tree, went through a fence and hit the concrete casing of a field pump. The truck was totaled. She was bruised, but unhurt. Ten days later, one of her horses nearly gouged his eye out—another inexplicable injury and another big vet bill. The vet saved his eye, but barely. He was going to need months of care and separation from the other horses. Barry helped her tend him, which was a good thing, because her horse was wild with pain and she was in no shape to tend him herself. One evening, Barry turned loose of him too soon and Marcia got knocked to the ground as the horse careened to get away from their ministrations. She lay against the wall looking up at her husband and her horse wondering why all of this was happening. Her formerly calm horse stood against the far wall regarding her with a cold eye. She stood up to go to him, but froze and she saw his flattened his ears. Barry grabbed her arm and pulled her out of the stall. He guided her into the house and walked her up the stairs to bed. "I just don't understand anything."

The physical work that week was agony; she got more sore for three days running. Barry dutifully took care of the farm and her horses while she was at work, but she could see the strain in him. It seemed like a live wire was running through the herd, making every one of them agitated for no apparent reason.

One night when she couldn't sleep, she tiptoed down the stairs to the kitchen. She fixed herself some tea and sat alone at the table, feeling empty and sad.

Later that week, a piece of equipment nearly fell on Barry when he was out by himself working on the tractor. That evening after dinner, she grabbed her coat and went out to survey the scene. She could see exactly what had happened and nearly happened. A chill ran up her spine and over her skull. The thought of him being pinned, or worse, with no one to come to his aid made her feel faint.

The following week, she went into her manager's office and started the paperwork for her resignation. He tried to talk her out of it, reminding her how close she was to vesting, but she said that what was at stake at home was more important than a supplemental income later on. She was walking away from about 2200 dollars a month that would kick in 20 years when she reached the age of 55. That sum of money would not matter now and probably would not matter at all in 20 years. Barry had a knack for making money and investing. He had not been exaggerating when he'd told her she didn't need to work. When Marcia told Barry she would be a full time wife in three weeks, he leapt to his feet, grabbed her and tried to spin, but nearly dropped her because of his injury. She groaned too because she was still sore from wrecking her truck and getting knocked down in the stall. "What a pair!" he laughed.

She was flooded with relief and things seemed to calm down.

Once she was free of her job, she dedicated herself to being a house wife. She got to walk out to wherever Barry was working and bring him hot coffee something out of the oven. She got to see her horses several times a day. Life was good.

One morning, she was upstairs cleaning when she heard Barry come in the back door and bellow her name. One of her horses had busted down a gate and was loose on the road. She flew outside and got to her horse before he got out on the road. A close call. A freak occurrence, and not at all like her horses. She put him in another pasture and went to help Barry fix the gate. When she got to him, he glared at her and threw down his tools, "you can start cleaning up after these nags now."

She apologized and worked on the gate for two hours. Barry didn't say a word to her the rest of the day. Or the next day. She was in the house when she heard a loud report and a horse scream. She ran to the back door to see Barry and Lester explode out of the barn in opposite directions. Barry had a broken 2 by 4 in his hands. He strode into the tractor barn and slammed the door. Marcia stood frozen for several minutes, then ran to the barn to see what she could see. Blood on a post. She went out into the pasture and located Lester in a far corner. She was halfway to him when she heard Barry yell her name. "He's okay. He ran past me and broke a board."

She waved at him and continued. He yelled again and she thought she heard an obscenity, but pretended not to hear him. The garage door slammed again.

Lester had a foot-long gash in his chest which was bleeding profusely. She could see the whites of his eyes. In six months, each of her horses had been injured and her truck destroyed. Why were they all having such bad luck? Were Barry's horses really beating up on hers or was something else going on?

That evening they had their first real argument. Marcia knew they disagreed about some things and held differing opinions about others, none of which concerned her or affected their relationship. Barry unloaded on her with a fury that scared her. He raged about everything--her cooking, her butt, her horses, her truck, her lovemaking, her baking. She sat dumbfounded and unable to respond. When he was finished, he stormed upstairs and slammed the bedroom door.

She cleaned up the kitchen, then sat in the study for hours before daring to go upstairs to bed. When at last she did, she found the bedroom door locked.

In the ensuing months, Barry took one of her horses to a show 800 miles away and withheld water the entire time. Bud collapsed in the arena and had to be dragged out with a tractor. They put him in a stall and he died there that night. Barry did not tell Marcia until he got home without her horse.

As Barry's verbal rampages intensified and her horses continued to have unexplained sicknesses and injuries, Marcia decided to leave. Barry had put her on an allowance so it took time for her to ferret away enough money to get away from him. She had lost touch with most of her friends and didn't feel she could call on them for help.

When Barry went to the next out-of-town show, she loaded up her belongings and her horses and left. She drove 500 miles south and moved in to a house his family owned. It didn't take him 10 minutes to figure out where she'd gone once he got back to town and found her gone.

She began divorce proceedings and tried to get a restraining order, but couldn't because he hadn't threatened to kill her, which was the criteria. He turned off her cell phone and stalked her. She had to get a job and feared for her horses' safety when she was at work. She took a job as a retail clerk for eight dollars an hour and wondered how she would survive. She also wondered what she had been thinking when she'd given up her job at FedEx before vesting in her pension.

Barry stalked Marcia for seven years. He called her at work so many times her employer reprimanded her, he defrauded her in the divorce, he got away with forging her signature on debt instruments that had been in his name, which ruined her credit, he set fire to her garage and he would have tried to kill more of her horses except they wouldn't come near him and he knew better than to try to go after them in the open pasture.

In the 10 years since she got away from Barry, Marcia has endured many hardships as a result of her decision to marry him and all that followed. She has lived at or below the poverty level and become an alcoholic. She still has her beloved horses, but struggles to care for them. She keeps them because they are old and she does not trust the horse market. They are her responsibility and her only joy. They have all healed from their physical wounds, but their hearts and lives will never be the same. Marcia has decided that when her last horse dies, she will die, too since she has nothing left and life is so unkind.

8 Behind the Mask

Of course, no woman in her right mind would willingly admit a predator into her life. This is why the psychopath adopts a persona and wears a mask. He uses it to befriend, help, earn trust, fascinate and flatter, all of which he does with perfect pitch. This social predator has an uncanny ability to read his prey and fashion his pursuit to be highly effective. Once the prey is under control (committed, compromised, exhausted, trapped, pressured), the games begin. The psychopath begins to reveal his true nature: joking turns into humiliation, criticism turns into character assassination, sex turns into sadism, demands turn into degradation and more. Being on the receiving ends of these private revelations is highly destabilizing. It is the betrayal of trust by the one you trusted most. All of this works to increase your vulnerability. You don't understand, you want things to go back to how they were, so you try harder. This is how the initial wounds buy him more time and set you up to for more pain. Too few women know what these behaviors mean and fewer still are able to react to avert further damage.

Emotional states of extreme anxiety, especially laced with fear and horror, make you more impressionable and more vulnerable; this is why women who have been entrapped by psychopaths often exist in a sort of trance. When mental and emotional coping mechanisms get overwhelmed, they go into overdrive at first, they go numb and then they shut down from exhaustion—which sets them up for even worse predation. It's a vicious circle. Some women seek help, others do not.

The man and woman in an abusive relationship both function in different sorts of denial about what is really taking place between them—both are in denial about what he is, what he is doing to her and how the abuse is affecting her.

Since most psychopathy is created by genes or early childhood trauma, there is often partial or total lack of acknowledgment from the family, too. The parents, siblings and children of psychopaths wrote the book on "flanking" or protectively surrounding the psychopath and denying his abuse. Let anyone question the behavior or inquire into the background of the psychopath and you will see them close ranks and flare off. When a psychopath is on trial, you will see his family in the courtroom decrying his accusation and proclaiming his innocence.

Most psychopaths get by with their intimate crimes; they know how to stay inside the law or outside detection for what they do. When suspicions are raised, they change locations, spouses, territories or methodologies. Of course, none of this lessens their pathology.

To the uninitiated, the psychopath is taken at face value. The prey responds to the promises made implicitly and explicitly by the persona. These promises are crafted to be irresistible to the prey. The psychopath uses his best manners to be smooth and charming, even to the point of being unctuous. He or she is seldom mannerly, shy or inclined to observe social conventions except during the entrapment phase.

Learning to look for particular tendencies and behavior patterns is the key to seeing through the appealing mask used by a dangerous predator. Learning to see the following behaviors in their earliest

The Angry Partner

His use of anger is calculated and corrosive, which blunts healthy release and the flow of remedial energies. Like alcohol, anger is a convenient and convincing excuse for loss of self control. The pathological uses the display and threat of outburst to control his victim, to instill fear, doubt while also delivering the deep wounds of minimization and insult. The payoff for him is the emotional and practical damage his outbursts inflict and the chilling effect they have in the aftermath.

The pathological use of anger is corrosive to the spirit. It is out of all proportion to reason and reality. He blows up at the slightest thing or at nothing at all, making anger an unpredictable weapon. The pathological use of anger has none of the remedial characteristics of healthy anger expressions, which can help resolve problems and bring two people closer. Instead, the victim is kept off balance, kept scared, made to feel inadequate and helpless, all of which work against her need to think clearly so she can get help.

You miss an exit on the highway. Instead of letting you make the needed correction without comment, he becomes enraged.

His anger displays may range from annoyance to fury. They can be a shock to witness and terrifying to receive. His first reaction to the slightest infraction is anger.

You water the plants too much or not enough, you leave water drops on the counter and he erupts with rage.

You put an object on a shelf instead of into a drawer, or vice versa. When he discovers this mistake he bludgeons you with it.

His primary problem with anger was likely seeded in him when he was a very young child. It is now a learned behavior that he knows how to use at will to control and terrorize. The controlling behaviors he expresses through anger cause physical and emotional harm right then and there and in years to come.

His outbursts may be followed with apology or contrition, albeit without sincere accountability.

He may apologize for his less threatening displays while making no remark at all about his full-blown eruptions.

He may say you make him "lose control" when in fact in his wrath he is trying to "take control" of you.

He may deny or minimize all of his behaviors.

There are two sides to this red flag: his suppressed (undirected) anger at "something" and his expressed (directed) anger at you. Among other things, his anger can be an expression of his belief about his role in the relationship and his reaction when it is breached. The pathological believes he is above reproach and above rules: he alone is justified. When you get angry yourself or even merely object to his anger, he responds with rage. So, you learn to maintain a poker face, squash your feelings, edit your words and stifle self expression to avoid his wrath. This muting of the self is an act of self preservation, but it is not healthy. In the long term, it is debilitating.

The stress of living with a human volcano takes a heavy toll on your health that should not be underestimated. It can cause a range of visible health problems as well as many that don't show, for a while. Rash, headaches and stomach aches are common, so are adrenal and lymphatic exhaustion. Victims of abuse are known to suffer heart attack and stroke later on. Anger displays (and threats) occur along a continuum, from mild to extreme; likewise, the reactions it elicits from you can range from a slight startle to utter terror.

There is raw power in the honest expression of healthy anger. He may know this, at least subconsciously, and he has a vested interest in keeping you from accessing that power. The pathological partner does not want his victim to have anything, not even her own power.

The Dangerous Driver Partner

Road rage is one barometer of the extent of his sickness. Normal people sometimes do things behind the wheel they would never do to someone's face. Roads offer a Driving may be the behavior that first reveals his hidden nature. Despite the inherent risk of acting out while behind the wheel of thousands of pounds of metal and fuel, people sometimes act out in traffic ways they would never behave in person.

Road rage is a dangerous, immature, selfish and extremely hostile set of learned behaviors. It is an outburst that can often be indulged in without consequence.

He honks at, cuts in front of and tails cars that get in his way.

He makes obscene gestures and yells at other drivers.

He passes other vehicles when it is dangerous and illegal to do so.

He assumes he has the right of way in all circumstances and gets provoked when challenged.

He becomes enraged if he encounters other drivers who drive the way he does.

These behaviors can erupt for the slightest reason or for no reason at all. A man who exhibits road rage is showing you:
- His lack of concern for safety.
- His willingness to do harm.
- His need to get his way.
- His intolerance of others.
- The lengths to which he'll go to terrorize you.

If you have a history of car crashes or you are just a nervous passenger, you can be sure he'll make use of that fact for his own purposes every time you get in the car with him. Being trapped in a speeding car with an out-of-control driver is a form of torture. He knows this.

Note: According to the National Safety Council there were over 36 thousand traffic fatalities, over six million injuries and costs in excess of 200 billion dollars on American roads because of car crashes in 2012.

How many of these are caused by deliberate acts of road rage where a psychopath is behind the wheel?

The Cheating Partner

You can be sure everything he said to you, he has said and will say to countless other women.

The abusive individual at core is predatory; for many such men, other women are just prey items—outlet for gratification. There is no love or affection involved, just ego stroking and hot but impersonal sex.

Other women supply him with content for threats (expressed or insinuated) to his wife or girlfriend. In all likelihood, he has at least one other woman on the hook at all times. Continuous predation allows him to perfect his game. He feels entitled to and justified in his pursuit of other women, even if he is married.

If he is young, he brags about it to his peers, if he is older, he has learned to hide it and lie about it.

Other women are his favorite compulsion. He could no more give it up than he could quit breathing. If he lives in a small town, he may be forced to look elsewhere for women. The easiest place to hunt for prey is the unlimited pool of willing women on the internet. He may be registered with one dating or sex service or with many. He may be a novice user or an accomplished predator. Preying on women on the internet is easy because it gives him free rein while assuring his anonymity and providing abundant free feedback on his methodology. He may use the same profile, messages and methods with hundreds of women.

People often behave while driving in ways they would not dare behave face-to-face. This same principle applies to conduct on the internet.

This type of man tends to be methodical, so the internet dating world is easy for him to systematize, which gives him a lot of leverage and practice. He perfects his pitch all the time; he has learned what to lead with and what kind of bait to use for the kind of woman he wants.

He has developed the knack for finding and engaging nice, trusting women who quickly fall under his spell. He is especially adept at dispelling the doubts that this kind of woman is sure to have if he does encounter her on the internet:

"Don't worry, I am not a player."

"I'm a one-woman man."

"Obviously, I am seriously looking for a long-term or permanent relationship."

Whether he hunts for women on the internet, in the paper, in bars or just in town, he likely uses the same general operating procedure, tailored for every woman he makes contact with. He plays the varied roles with aplomb. If he hooks up with or marries one of these women, his predation is seldom interrupted for long. He is back online as soon as the honeymoon is over because he is incapable of love and unable to take any woman seriously.

As he secures you, he continues to keep other prospects in the background so he can develop them and play with them on an as-needed basis. He may even taunt you with this information later to force your hand in some way. Like sex, his other women pursuits are important to him, but none of it is lasting, personal or sacred because he is empty inside. He has nothing to offer except the sex act, which is likely unremarkable. Other women are just a routine by which he gratifies his need to control and destroy. That's what he really gets off on.

The Compulsive Partner

His compulsions surround you like a desert landscape—no variety, no relief, no nourishment, no hope.
The more toxic the abuser, the more compulsive his behavior. He is driven by private urges, worn routines and inflexible opinions. One of the characteristics that feeds the compulsion of the psychopathic partner is insatiability. Whatever he has or does, he wants more.

If he's a charismatic con artist that preys on women, his predations must feed his insatiable ego and sexual appetite.

If he's a financial con man, he has the money disease and is driven to defraud to quench his hunger for money.

If he has succeeded in his work life and is in a position of power or influence, he is compelled to have his woman subordinate to him and at his beck and call.

The ruthlessness of psychopaths allows them to succeed in business and competitive pursuits, so many of them have the resources to insist on and persist with their predation to an uncommon degree. Whatever his age, he is set in his ways and used to getting his way. He knows how to wear his compulsions so that they appear as extraordinary disciplines or high passions—at first. He uses them to awe and attract—at first. Later, he will reveal them to be weapons of coercion which he uses at will against his partner physically, mentally, emotionally, financially.

His compulsion is your coercion. He is rigid about how certain things are to be done and the burden of performance is on you. Chances are none of it matters at the end of the day, but the routines are required nevertheless. Being "employed" in the fulfillment of someone else's compulsions can become mind-numbing and soul-deadening by virtue of the pointless repetition alone. Day in. Day out. Over and over. Ad nauseum. No creativity. No spontaneity. No satisfaction. No choice.

His compulsion about cleanliness could mean you spend many of your waking hours dusting, washing, wiping, scrubbing and so forth.

His compulsion about order could mean you have to memorize the exact placement of every object in every room of the house.

His compulsion about sex could mean you have to submit to certain activities at night before you can go to sleep or in the morning before you can get out of bed.

His compulsion about money could mean he controls it and you have little or none or you live like you have none.

Compulsion introduces a measure of unreality into daily life. Trivial things are made oppressively important. Everyday tasks are made intrusive and burdensome. You are not to ask why. You are not allowed to have any preferences or priorities of your own. You are simply to capitulate. There is no let-up. He adds to his compulsions at will. Any new object or event presents an opportunity for a new compulsion. In his mind, his compulsions are your duties to him. They are endless, pointless, petty and tedious.

The Egotistical Partner

It's all about him and it will always be all about him. Egotism derives from an inflated sense of self in relation to the rest of the world and an immature perspective— both come from delusions of grandeur and shallowness. The young abuser tends to be arrogant and egotistical; the older abuser cloaks his arrogance with false humility. Some psychologists say that psychopaths are unable to learn from their experience except in ways that serve them in the moment. This may have to do as much with their insatiability as it does with their lack of self control.

The predator refines his methods with each new opportunity, but despite this, his predation exposes him and he is run out of (another) town (job) because of the number of women he's victimized there.

Every abuser has his own style: he may strut about like a young buck, be the strong, silent type, the reserved retiree at church or play some other role. Whatever face he shows in public does not betray the enormous ego inside. He has carefully cultivated his mask(s) over time to ensure he keeps his outward appearance and reputation to serve his predation by serving his persona. The way that the abuser cloaks his ego is telling—the way he presents himself in public provides clues about two things, the way he thinks of himself and the way he wants his ego fed. For example, the young buck wants to impress and be admired, the strong, silent type wants to awe and be sought, the reserved retiree wants to magnetize and be adored.

The bottom line about the egotism of the pathological partner is that it does not conform with the way he initially presented himself to you.

If you responded to his mask, chances are he did a good job of hiding his predatory nature and his egotism. If he is an experienced abuser, all of this may have gotten by you because he has become so proficient in hiding his true nature and reeling in his victims. When you fall for the mask, your emotions fail you by keeping you from seeing the monster behind it.

Delusions of grandeur infuse the abuser's egotism. Although he thinks well of himself, he knows to lead with his strong suit according to the prey he is trying to bring down; that is, he puts forward the qualities he knows you will notice and respond to, based on his observations. For example, if you are financially burdened, he leads with his financial strength and offers to help relieve some of your burdens. If you are struggling with a difficult child, he leads with his paternal prowess and offers to spend time with the child. If you were dealing with a difficult boss or landlord, he leads with his diplomatic mind and offers counsel or mediation.

As a shallow, superficial person, he thinks of himself as a fine figure of a man and a great catch for any woman, but he doesn't admit this up front. Instead, he says his success is due to the fact that things come easily to him, his great upbringing, hard work or luck.

There is little chance of any mention of something going wrong on his watch—ever—unless it's caused by someone else. This lack of accountability is a function of egotism and in the extreme, a hallmark of psychopathy. His initial easy-going ways and self-deprecating humor are carefully crafted and delivered to be charming, disarming and engaging. And they are— for a while.

He is self centered, but not self aware.

He is his own little "g" god.

He is consumed with getting his own needs met.

He pursues his wants to the exclusion of all else.

Among other things, his life may be constructed to serve his pleasure seeking and enhance his well being. And that's where you come in. You are the embodiment of his security, ego-building faculty. Your job is to feed and enlarge his ego by being his "Yes" woman, by attending to his every whim and by being his audience 24/7.

The pathological he spends an inordinate amount of his personal resources on himself. If he is getting on in years, his pursuit of the fountain of youth may be nothing short of spectacular.

- Grooming himself
- Improving his health or fitness
- Planning his entertainments
- Shopping for new possessions
- Playing with his 'toys'
- Surrounding himself with trophies
- Making improvements to his home
- Fussing over himself and his things

If illness or injury befalls him, it dominates your waking hours until he has recovered. There is no mishap too insignificant when it happens to him. If he stubs his toe or loses a button, you hear about it for weeks or months.

The Enslaving Partner

Rights are soon things you only remember.

In the beginning, he looks after your every need. He acts chivalrous, considerate, sensitive and mannerly. This doesn't last long. In an abusive relationship, one person has rights and the other person has none.

These are some of the first to go once the gloves come off:

Freedom to defend yourself

Freedom from damage to and loss of your property

Freedom to express yourself

Freedom from arbitrary actions

Freedom to exercise your own judgment
A healthy relationship allows and enriches each person's freedoms, often without the need for extensive discussion or negotiation. Each person retains their self determination, which they adjust willingly because they love their partner, not because they are coerced. This is what you expect and this may be how it starts. It all just works, but because abusive relationships are counterfeit, you eventually discover that what it is, is not what it appeared to be.

As he manipulates circumstances to acquire more control the balance of power shifts. You have some awareness of this, but you don't realize it's the prelude to abuse. You chalk it up to your inexperience, or lack of confidence, you tell yourself it's just the give-and-take of relationships. The things you notice seem too insignificant to bring up. You decide to rise above them, and you do, for a while.

The amount of space your things occupy in the house shrinks.

The amount of freedom you have to come and go is restricted, implicitly or explicitly.

The amount of respect shown for your feelings and needs is minimal, even grudging.

Your access to your children, animals or property may be made conditional upon your behavior so that it is diminished, threatened or eliminated.

If you are financially dependent on him or married to him, you will watch as your rights disappear. When he doesn't have to be bothered with considering you at all, everything is so much easier for him. If you still love him, you may be able to face the fact that your love has been lied to, your trust has been deceived, your vulnerability exploited and your force spent. It is the 21st century and your rights have been removed. As your life becomes less and less, it's harder and harder to believe you are worthy.

You are never given a car key, a house key or a check book.

You are told not to lock the bathroom door and he tests it.

Your absences from him are timed and monitored.

You are to start dinner immediately after coming in work.

You are not to question why he sits around all day like his arms are broken and whines about being alone and having nothing to do.

While you were doing dishes, he was sitting back letting time work to his advantage. He is breaking you in and wearing you down. He's been down this road before. Once your resources were gone, he took you over like a warlord. He has usurped everything. You can't believe what he is doing to you as he is doing it to you. Eventually, you begin to believe you don't deserve any rights. Most days, you are too exhausted and numb to care about the losses you live with. You may accept the position he's put you in. Your head is filled with self-blame and self-doubt—that he put there and that you allowed. The removal of rights is just one way to rub salt in the universal wound of "I'm not good enough."

The Entitled Partner

He thinks you are there to be consumed by him.
Entitlement is not by definition a negative thing, but
when twisted or taken to extremes, it becomes harmful.
Some feel one of the root causes of abusive relationships
is a warped sense of personal entitlement. This can be
attributed to DNA, patriarchal society or cultural
conditioning. Some of the most advanced civilizations
on earth have succeeded because the male went out into
the world to hunt, legislate, fight and earn a living while
the female stayed home to raise children, keep the home
and nurture her mate.

It's not hard to see how emotionally immature or
socially undeveloped males could exploit this situation
to the point of abusing their wives. In some cultures for
example, a female is not permitted to leave the house
without being accompanied by a male relative. This
requirement assumes that the female and males at large
are untrustworthy and might engage in illicit behavior
without the presence of a protective male.

A review of the roles that males have fulfilled through
history as well as current statistics show that males are
more inclined than females to engage in acts of
aggression (including sexual aggression), whether it be
sparring with a co-worker, challenging a competitor or
dominating his wife.

Cultural observations have identified certain pressure
points that can trigger this aggression in behaviors that
express an entitlement mindset. When ill-expressed,
such as through deceit and domination, entitlement is
actually an abnegation of responsibility rather than the
assumption of responsibility. It is a highly assumptive

mindset that is not based on a reality in which fairness, logic and justice apply. This is the playing field of the psychopathic and the possessed.

In the beginning, entitlement can be expressed in ways that are unique and appealing, such as by conveying a man's masculinity and prowess. He carries himself with confidence; he lives with zeal and high expectation. This self assurance makes his choice of you thrilling—at first. His ways are winning. His energies impress. If he has had success in his work endeavor, you may suppose that his confidence and sense of entitlement are two reasons for it. Taken as a whole, the early signs of entitlement can reflect well on him and on you.

As the relationship proceeds, he begins to turn that zeal, expectation and sense of entitlement on you. It may seem that the quality of his attention changes overnight into something else. You begin to see things that cause you to question his emotional maturity. Something is coming forth that does not consider you—it is not considerate, appropriate or fair. As it creeps into more and more of your space and the relationship, you begin to feel crowded and pushed around by this thing that is out of all proportion to reality.

Because he believes he deserves whatever he wants, his demands begin to increase in number and complexity; they occupy more and more of your time, energy and emotions.

Some of your duties and many shared activities exist only to feed his ego.

Like double standards and hypocrisy, he seems to be unaware of the unfairness and recklessness of his behavior and the ways in which it affects you. This could be due to denial and narcissism. Pushing his sense of entitlement on you doesn't have anything to do with loving you; it's all about his need to sate his insatiability.

He says he's entitled to having his way about something because he knows more about it than you do or because he's wanted longer or more than you or because he deserves it more than or because he supports you.

The plain truth is that he believes he is entitled to whatever he wants, including you. His entitlement is all-encompassing and he is quick to deny or justify its encroachment if challenged. Unchecked entitlement can turn into usurpation, where he takes over your life.

• *He sets himself up as the sole authority in the relationship so he can function as a little "g" god.*

• *He believes he has the right to dominate you to achieve his purposes.*

• *He overrules you.*

• *He uses weasel words to play on your emotions.*

• *He expects you to agree with him and bullies you if you do not.*

• *If he persuades you to enter into an agreement with him, he swears that it's mutually beneficial, but you will find it turns you into a prisoner.*

• *There is a lot of smallness and sameness in daily life, except for the misery, which grows and twists.*

• *His entitlements expand and grow exponentially until your energy is sapped and you collapse.*

An entitlement mindset expresses elements of lower behaviors that are repressed until the romance has got you in the trap. Once you've been seduced into the "deal" the encroachments and taking and usurpation begin. Entitlement can be implemented sexually, financially, emotionally, socially, physically and so forth. It can go on until you are drained of resources, life force and vital energy.

Finally, the entitlement flag is not unlike cooking a frog. You put it in cold water so it doesn't protest and then you turn the heat on. You cook it slowly. By the time the frog realizes it's in trouble, it's too far gone to escape.

The Hypocritical Partner

He's a back slapper and a back stabber.

His being and doing give mixed messages. He describes and thinks of himself as one sort of person but behaves in the opposite way compounding the distress of his partner.

Hypocrisy is another form of emotional dishonesty that reveals lack of conscience, immaturity and shallowness. This man does not walk his talk. His talk drips with largesse and passion, while his walk is mean and indifferent. It's not that he's acting, it's that he's empty. Hypocrisy runs on emotional dishonesty in its many forms. In the abusive individual, these qualities exist with an attenuated conscience as well.

He tells you he's a one-woman man, but later reveals himself to be a habitual philanderer.

He tells you he's an honest man, but you later learn he has lied to you and others pathologically.

He tells you he's sensitive, yet he treats you cruelly.

He gives you books to read so that you will be a better partner to him, but refuses to do likewise himself.

He tells you he's a people person, but you rarely witness him say or do a kind thing for anyone else.

He tells you he's a family man, but he has unhealthy or superficial relationships with family members.

He may use other behaviors and tactics in his hypocrisies. Blaming, denying, lying, minimizing and withholding information are all enabling and useful to the hypocrite.

When a neighbor calls to ask a small favor, he doesn't go to the door or answer the phone. When he runs into the neighbor later, without flinching, he says how sorry he is he wasn't home or never got the message. He may even blame you for failing to relay the message!

If he does do something for you, no matter how minor, he will talk it up for months as if it is one of the greatest, most heroic, most self-sacrificial gifts a man ever gave his woman.

Whatever he may have promised you, he is quick to forget or take away. In this way, his hypocrisy can be cruelly employed. Hypocrisy serves the speaker of weasel words well.

"I was not put on this earth to take care of you."

"You can go back where you came from."

"I don't owe you a thing."

He requires profuse thanks and regular apologies from you all the while he denies your experiences and refuses to give you any thanks or apology you are due. The message to you is clear: your feelings do not matter and you do not matter outside of enabling him to gratify himself. If he asked you to quit your job, leave your business or otherwise deplete your own financial resources to pursue the relationship with or get married to him, he does not hesitate to threaten you with abandonment or expulsion if your efforts don't live up to his expectations. In fact, he derives pleasure from roaring at you to get out of his house knowing that you have no way to escape him.

The Immature Partner

He's as grown up as he'll ever be—the mind of a 14-year old in a man's body.

His immaturity can be breathtaking. Regardless of his age and life experience, his behavior shows that his emotional maturity was arrested a long time ago. The way he spends his time can provide insight about the nature and extent of his immaturity. He is more or less a child in an adult's body. His devices and maladjustments are the adult manipulations of a child's anxieties.

However he acts out, his immaturity will express itself in:

- Shallowness
- Vindictiveness
- Inconsistency
- Instability
- Meanness
- Selfishness
- Hyper-reactiveness
- Inattentiveness
- Immorality
- Insatiability
- Infidelity

- Violence

No matter what situation you find yourself in with him, you cannot count on him to be mature, fair, predictable, stable, thorough or reliable. This is not due to his lacking these life skills or being unable to use them, this is due to his being unwilling to use them in his relationship with you. You can be sure he uses diplomacy at work and out in public, but when he gets home to you, he tosses consideration and reverts to type. Part of the role of the woman in an abusive relationship can be likened to a sort of mothering—but mothering as it was never meant to be. When your partner is abusive, the relationship is unbalance and unhealthy. All emotional enrichment and nourishment comes from you. All apology, patience, willingness to forbear, compassion, forgiveness, supplication comes from you. Whether it's sex, forgiveness, another chance or self sacrifice you give, he takes. He demands, you supply. He may express his immaturity in ways to make you feel sorry for him. This is base manipulation. Feeling sorry for him is a trap.

He mopes or sulks extravagantly.

He refuses to talk.

He slams doors.

He eats alone.

He closes himself off in a room.

He drives off in a rage.

He bellows when he doesn't get his way.

He threatens you to compel performance.

His emotional maturity is hopelessly stuck at the level of a child or adolescent. He possesses very little emotional depth if any, and in all truth, is a consistently demanding and draining partner in an intimate relationship.

The Immoral Partner

Immorality is an easy way out. It requires no character. It gives nothing, but takes everything—except the high road.

Immorality is the absence of morality, which is defined as "a system of reliable conduct based on principles of uprightness."

In a relationship, morality is expressed by a baseline of behaviors that are fair and honest, that bequeath a reasonable expectation of a person who is guided by their conscience to do the right thing, even when no one is looking.

As discussed, brain-damaged psychopaths are rendered without conscience, are not disposed to do the right thing (unless it serves them) and display a host of behaviors that exhibit immorality. The absence of conscience and attendant immorality enable them to remain unconcerned about the deficits they cannot detect. They are comfortable with and well served by their immorality. Their mindset is focused on their gratification, no matter the cost to others. The mindset of the non-psychopathic abuser fluctuates between getting away with abuse when he can and trying to do better the next time.

Society is awash in messages that feed baser instincts from demanding bosses to violent media which often lead people to a choice between the lesser of two evils. These add up to implied norms that condone laxity, selfishness and disrespect. These evolving ideas have dovetailed enough to light a fuse which will explode into social chaos as those most vulnerable turn into parasitical and predatory creatures. Interpersonal abuse is at plague level now and it will continue to increase unless something changes.

Except for blatant opportunistic predation, an abusive individual may not display his immorality, except to perhaps to drop hints about whatever he most wants from you. He is charming and appealing, which hides his dishonesty. He is adept at something and he uses that to gain advantage. He is funny, he has some expertise, he raps, he drives fast backwards, he dances, he does card tricks, he picks pockets and so forth to entertain, to build affinity, to gain access. He is a smooth talker.

If he is in a position that requires persuasive selling, he is very successful. He could sell an igloo to an arctic dweller, he could have talked the pilgrims out of their provisions before they left port and he could talk you out of your life.

He is convincing because he has been lying for so long he believes his own fictions. He has no awareness of the immorality of manipulating you and he is so good at it that you don't question him for a while. As he wins your trust and gains access to your inner life and your home, he plays you and sizes you up at the same time. It's a relationship to you, but it's just a game to him. He is there to take, you are there to give.

He rushes you to be sexually intimate by playing the sort of man you most want him to be.

He carefully inquires into your assets.

He finds out who your closest friends are.

He identifies your vulnerabilities, physical, mental, emotional, financial, spiritual, etc.

He takes careful note of your deepest emotional wound.

It is fun and exciting. There is "something" about him. He pushes you in some ways and you go along because you like it. When you give in to him, you tell yourself you're growing and pushing your limits. Sometimes when you are alone you feel an undercurrent of resentment, but the next time he walks in the room, it vanishes. His "something" keeps you engaged. You always want more of him than you get. He keeps you hungry and you wonder if it's on purpose to draw you farther out.

He is adventurous and daring; he can play conventional or unconventional convincingly. He lives by his own rules. He avoids the things that pain him and gives in every time to the things that tempt him. He courts the forbidden and let it hold sway over him. When his mind says he must have her or it, he does. He is his sole authority.

If his primary temptation is sex, you may find yourself carrying one or more infectious diseases.

If his primary temptation is drugs, you may find your house vulnerable to a drug bust.

If his primary temptation is money, you may be cleaned out or expected to participate in a heist.

Then, there begin to be incidences. They will test your patience and your boundaries. They may seem spontaneous, but they have likely been time-tested on dozens of other victims.

He forgets to put gas in your car after using it.

He doesn't give your kids their snack when they get home from school.

He leaves the gate open; your dog(s) get out of the yard and get hit by a truck.

He doesn't return your _____ that he had to borrow.

He forgets to give you your mail and your phone messages.

He deposits your check into his account.

He books himself on a trip without telling or including you.

He apologizes or makes excuses. You either accept them and things go on or you don't and things change. Things change when you draw your line in the sand. Even if there's not a confrontation, he will feel it when his ways are beginning to grate. If you're not married to him, chances are he will take or keep what he wants and leave.

The Indifferent Partner

Indifference is the sign of an emotional amputee.
In the beginning, he displays the ability to be laid-back and take in stride the stresses of life. Later, his partner sees that he does not take things in stride, at least not with her, when she finds herself on the receiving end of a vicious tirade and she realizes with no small amount of shock that he's not laid-back—he's indifferent, even unfeeling.

He is largely unaffected by and uninterested in other people's experience and personhood.

If he reacts at all, it is with indifference or impatience.

He shows no compassion or empathy for others because he feels none.

He expresses hot impatience when another person's situation, no matter how grave, poses even the most minor inconvenience to him.

If another driver is slow to respond, he honks and gives him the finger instead of driving around him or waiting for the other driver to act.

You cannot depend upon him to look after your animals or children because he is indifferent to their existence. He does not care if they are safe and comfortable. Indifference is said to be the opposite of love and a second cousin to aversion. The more outright indifference an abuser displays, the more he demonstrates the extent of his emotional limitations. In public, he knows he must feign compassion and concern, and he plays this part to perfection. He knows he has to make a show of catering to you in front of other people. His loving husband act is convincing to others. But in private, he reverts to type.

He may inquire of your comfort on a cold night, but then refuse to let you put another blanket on the bed.

He may ask you what entrée you'd like to have at a restaurant, but then tell you to order something else.

In private, he does not react normally to another person's suffering. He may not react at all or he may laugh.

He laughs when he sees a man pounding the steering wheel in his car while screaming at his wife who has her head in her hands.

If you get hurt and sustain a visible wound, he tells you to stay home so no one else sees it and to cover it up so he doesn't see it.

If you suffer a loss, even one which he causes, he offers no apology, comfort, condolence or help.

It may be wise to consider what he would do if you were ever badly hurt and he was the only person around. Plan accordingly.

The Injuring Partner

He feeds on your pain and suffering.
In a contest between male and female of same or similar age, there is little chance that she will be able to hold her own for even a few minutes, much less win the contest. The man who likes to hurt his woman knows this. There are men who batter their women, there are men who arrange accidents and there are men who inflict non-physical injuries.
In her 70s bestseller, THE WOMEN'S ROOM, Marilyn French wrote something like, "You don't have to murder a woman, you can just let her work in your office for 300 dollars a week."
The injuries that abusive men inflict on their women run the gamut and a third of the men that abuse are professionals who are well regarded in their communities as lawyers, bankers, teachers, doctors and pastors. Injury can mean disablement, maiming and death. A third of women who are abused by their husband or boyfriend never fully recover and a number

of them choose suicide to escape the pain. Extreme injuries can be sustained in any relationship. He may say, "But, I never hit her..." This is not the core issue. The core issue is his need to control her and the damage that does to her.

When you fall for a man, the last thing that crosses your mind is whether or not he would ever harm you or cause you to be harmed. Injury can take many forms—some seen, some unseen. Abusive relationships include multiple forms of abuse that inflict a variety of wounds. An abusive man knows there are lots of ways to hurt a woman that are not overtly physical, although they do a lot of damage. He knows he doesn't have to hit you or run over you or push you off a ledge to get you to do what he wants.

He can get you to quit your job or leave your business to impoverish you.

He can talk you out of buying or keeping a car to immobilize you.

He can get you to relocate with him to isolate you.

He can take away your animals to emotionally weaken you.

He can confuse and demean you to the point that you are second-guessing yourself and not thinking clearly.

He can tire you so much that you're having accidents around the house and getting hurt.

Then, he will deride you for being stupid and clumsy to drive home his general contention that you are unloved, unwelcome and unworthy. If he can lure you into bed, he will try to shame you. If he is a craven distempered type of psychopath, he injures you in bed.

He likes the rush of sex in strange places.

He likes the thrill of taking you against your will.

He flies into rages and vents himself sexually.

His demands leave you sore, torn, bleeding.
Many women who have been injured in various ways by their abusers report that physical injuries are easier to get over than non-physical injuries. A broken bone heals faster than a broken spirit. Nevertheless, at some point he may hurt you physically.

He rapes you.

He swings you into the sharp edge of a large piece of furniture.

He leaves something on the stair at night, like a tennis ball or a sharp rock.

He slams a door in your face or on your fingers accidentally on purpose.

He arranges something to break under or fall on top of you.

He causes a crashing noise when you are working with a large animal who could kick out in fright.

He locks you in the basement and turns off the heat because you are not communicative enough.

He locks you out of the house without anything but the clothes on your back because you gave a ride to a female friend.

Whether he does it directly or indirectly, you feel it just the same. You hide the damage—for a while because whatever his method, your injuries are minor at first. But, they become more serious because it takes more to satisfy him each time. If he is completely devoid of conscience, then there is no limit to the lengths he might go to gratify himself by hurting you. You may not be able to predict his methods and his weapons for hurting you, but you can bet whatever they are, they will be employed with more cunning and force to do more damage next time.

The time during which you are most vulnerable to attack (of any and all kinds) is when you are leaving and for the following six to nine months. Even if he has never laid a hand on you before, he could then.

The Insatiable Partner

The pathological is a woman-hating, woman-hurting junkie.

He is as consumed with getting his fix as any drug addict; he may be an addict in addition to being an abuser and use this as an excuse for his behavior if he is challenged. (But remember, he does not abuse because he is drunk or high, he abuses because he is mentally ill.) His fix comes from controlling and destroying his prey.

He is self centered, but not self aware. There is no such thing as enough for him. His careful withholding of needful things from his partner is in total contrast to his fiendish pursuit of whatever he wants and needs. When he discovers what he likes and how he can get it, there is no stopping him. Whether it is money, sex, drugs, power, property or sensation, once is not enough. A thousand is not enough. A million is not enough. When, in the course of his development as a toxic personality and the refinement of his "craft" he discovers what it is that makes his engine hum, his soullessness gets its first fix and his predation begins in earnest. His insatiability is fed by other personality dynamics, such as denial, delusions of grandeur, resistance to authority, irresponsibility and so forth. His insatiability can be of such magnitude that he seeks prey outside of his relationship with you. If his fix is sexual sadism, for example, he may have become a sex addict or a serial rapist. He will hide this from you as long as he needs to. His exertions will intensify over time in his quest for more and more gratification until his predations become lethal to one of his partners. He may have been raping her for hours, but he was so obsessed with himself that he did not notice she was losing consciousness or hemorrhaging.

As you're getting involved, you suspect none of this because you do not know better than to take him at face value. Besides, you're falling in love or you're married to him when the first big cracks in the mask appear. You are turned on by his vigor. You think his lust for life carries implicit promises for you of good things to come. You think the adventure, money or whatever he seeks will be shared with you. You think you can learn from him. The way he carries himself does not betray the insatiability that you have not seen yet.

He gets advancement at a work and gets off on the sensation of power. He goes to work behind the scenes undermining the next person in his way on his climb up the ladder.

He goes online for women. He develops a sequence of luring messages, which he uses on every willing prospect in this unlimited pool of victims. Over time, he sets up profiles at dozens of sites and has hundreds of women on the line at any given time.

In the beginning, you have no idea that this other side of him exists because you can't see the insatiability for what it is. His lies and manipulations are wrapped in romance or reason; this makes them more effective for him, but more compromising for you. Although you may do what he asks, it stings you.

Insatiability is a function of lack of conscience and soullessness. He directs a good portion of its energy into dispossessing you of what you have—this applies to tangibles and intangibles.

If you have close friends, he will not rest until he has relocated you or ruined those bonds.

If you have animals, he will go about taking them away from you.

If you have financial assets, he will use whatever influence he has with you to become involved and thereby begin to take control.

At the same time, his insatiability is at work getting, not just into your business, but into your mind. This is a big part of abuse: seizing control, separating you from your emotional and mental reserves and deriving pleasure from watching your suffering. An abuser takes you apart bit by bit, day by day. The more proficient he is as a predator, the less you will realize that you are being continually assessed and weakened by him. He may want to see what you know, what you think, how you have accomplished things in your own life or he may simply go about deleting the parts of your personality that do not feed him and replacing them with something else. This sort of usurpation is one of the ultimate aims of non-physical abuse—it takes you away from you. Remember, many predatory men go after high-functioning women precisely because they have the qualities required for him to run the con. The net effect of this is that your kindness, loyalty, etc., enables his insatiability, at least for a while.

He encourages you to get (more) fit by buying you clothes that are too small, withholding food, shaming you, hitting on athletic women, forcing you to exercise, etc.

He wants you to be a better wife and he is willing to assist you in this by giving you books to read, tapes to listen to. He points out women in movies or women on the street as examples of how he wants you to be.

If you don't challenge this, it becomes the norm and as such, is an indicator of his inability to feel compassion, guilt or shame.

He wants you to "be sexier."

He asks for more initiative in the bedroom.

He wants you to walk around the bedroom unclothed, then around the house, then outside.

He wants you to bathe with the bathroom door open.

He does not do any of these things, himself.
No matter what you concede to—and there are many reasons to concede, mental exhaustion being one of them—there is always more that is required. He is

unrelenting. He has an endless store of things he wants from you, things he wants you to do for him, attributes he wants to implant in your mind—most of all, he wants to see the suffering and waste he has wrought so he can gloat in the shambles of your life.

The Megalomaniac Partner

Rules are the necessaries of a small mind and a mean spirit.

In pathological relationships, there is often disturbing self-glorification by the abuser. He prides himself on his control of his partner, his antipathy, his manipulation of all things. As time takes its toll on the victim, she becomes more subdued; this makes it easier for him to express his pathology in ways that would have been intolerable to her at the beginning of the relationship. Rules have more impact on the victim in the early stages because the long-term effects of abuse have not yet blunted her spirit or poisoned her heart.

When one partner dominates a relationship through rules, the other partner resists, withdraws and finally goes numb. When the dominated partner has succumbed, the abuser is able to strut about in what he perceives to be the glory of his relentlessness and ruthlessness. He has no one to think about but himself. He is not restrained by guilt, shame or morality. His self centeredness gives him the feeling of omnipotent control, which is confirmed daily by his partner's fearful obedience and exhausted compliance.

Like every other form of abuse, rules are not in evidence or are so slight as to be small details in daily life. They can be communicated or demonstrated, like kicking off your shoes before going in the house or being careful not to slam the car door. They are so minor, you don't notice them or give them a second thought. Your thoughts are about him and your relationship with him. Shoes and car doors do not matter.

Things proceed. You fall for all of it, you get married or move in together. You don't know it yet, but few if any of the promises he's made and the agreements you've entered into will bear fruit. He begins to find ways of separating you from what you care about and he shows you that rules are a handy method for doing this.

If you have dog, he develops an allergy and makes a rule that the dog must stay outside whether it's 20 below or 120.

If you have a job, he decides that you must work less and makes a rule that if dinner isn't on the table by such-and-such a time, there will be trouble.

If you like to take walks, he will tell you when you can walk, where and for how long.

If you belong to a group, he announces he will attend a meeting and decide if you may continue in it.

As time goes by, the constriction is intentional and unmistakable. A dangerous element of a ruled relationship is its implied misogyny and disconnect from human decency. His rules express pettiness, vulgarity, egotism, greed and so on. Compared to the reasons you fell for this man, the reality you now face with him is void of the poetry of love. And even his rules about sex can't hide that.

Misogyny and violence are two indications that a relationship, and indeed a society, has turned. What seemed personal is impersonal, what seemed intimate is anti-social. What seemed wonderful is horrible. The counterfeit has been revealed. The normal behaviors of sharing food, making love, laughing and crying, running errands, etc., become grotesque aberrations of the simple joys of sharing your life with someone you love, respect and trust.

It crosses your mind that this is worse than being a slave because you can't get away from him, you can't go home for the night. The unwritten rule that underscores all the others is that he suffers you to be there. The feeling that comes through—if you can face it—is that he hates you. Daily life has been ground into powder. Every rule was introduced, one subtle change after another over time—like a political takeover—requested with reason and a smile, urged with propaganda and finally delivered with a threat of annihilation.

Rules for every room in the house.

Rules for every meal.

Rules for morning and rules for evening.

Rules for crumbs and rules for water spots.

Rules for phone calls and computer use.

Rules for folding towels and rolling socks.

Rules for going out and coming in.

Rules for smiling and for crying.

Rules for dressing and undressing.

Rules for sleeping and for waking.

The rules are all his and they are to be followed. In his mind, they are for his care and maintenance. They are for the smooth operation of the relationship and the running of the household according to him. The fact that it is all one-sided escapes him. Like rights, all benefits of the rules go to him.

Chances are, it may not be until someone else reacts to one of the rules you are observing that you see it. When you see it, you are thunder struck at the depth and breadth of the repression you've been living under. He has made the rules and he has reasons for each one of them. They express some of the worst fundamentals emerging from a postmodern society—normal people held hostage by the callous dramas of the morally insane.

The Tyrannical Partner

If he says "no", that's the end of it. If you say "no", that's the beginning of it.

Words are the most powerful thing in the universe and yet in the mouth of an abusive partner, even one who is not psychopathic or possessed, their power is misused. Some abusive individuals use words with astonishing skill to get what they want, but their actions show that words do not mean the same things to them as they do to normals.

In his landmark work, THE MASK OF SANITY, Hervey Cleckley, MD described a condition he called "semantic aphasia" as the inability to grasp the meaning of one's own words. He attributed this condition to primary psychopaths, who do not respond to disapproval and do not feel stress. Even though they are highly anti-social, they are cunning enough to control these impulses when it serves them. Lying, hypocrisy, double standards and manipulation are all in play when an abuser is awake.

When you're getting to know him, you see him deftly decline to take "no" for an answer. The way he pulls it off seems to be his turning a negative into a positive and you are impressed. You see him ask for special consideration and somehow get it.

He gets a restaurant to let him after hours.

He gets a free upgrade at a car rental.

He gets discount tickets not available to the public.

What you don't realize at first is that he charms and lies his way through life. What you also don't realize is that he does not like to take "no" for an answer. It costs him nothing to lean on service people to get more than he pays for, but if/when they say "no" to him, the stakes immediately become higher. He plays it like a game at first, but it gets ugly fast if it matters.

Over time, he begins to do this to you. The first time it happens, it may be over the pace of the relationship. He wants something that you don't want or are not ready for. He will charm, promise, lie, cajole, play, taunt to get you to compel. In the early part of the relationship, it will be fun and light. He will flatter and reassure. If you resist and stand your ground, the rules change.

Once you have stepped into the trap so that he has you, he won't take "no" for an answer, and he may or may not be nice about it. This should tell you two things:

•   He cares only about getting what he wants
•   You do not matter

If the relationship progresses, you discover that in his mind, only he is entitled to say "no". This is a red flag and this is one you would be wise to test early on.

As far as he's concerned, your job is to reply in the affirmative no matter what he asks of you. In his mind, you are not really you; you are his possession, his prey object. This is part of why problems arise when you express your true self by something as simple as saying "no."

You are there to gratify and indulge him.

You are there to reflect what he wants to see.

You are there to support what he wants to experience: himself in female form.

You do not have the right to deny him anything.

You do not have permission to express yourself.

You do not have the right to complain about or criticize anything.

Whenever it serves him, he will give lip service to your wants and needs but in truth, they do not matter and are not considered. Words do not matter or have meaning beyond getting him what he wants. He does not admit it, but this is what you come to realize after you have spent hours explaining, pleading or reminding him of his words. It is all for naught. There is no level playing field and your eloquence is wasted on his emptied soul.
The first few times you say "no", he acts accepting, perhaps with a little incredulity thrown in for good measure.
Later on, he'll respond to a "no" from you as an act of war.
He rejects it outright or he launches a counter-attack to demand you do whatever you've declined.
To assure the outcome he wants, he'll maneuver circumstances to force you if need be.
He does not hesitate to threaten you if you don't comply and will sabotage your work or kill your cat to make sure you get the message.
He does not deal well with any form of external authority, adversity or inconvenience. He cannot tolerate

complaint or critical comment from anyone although he dispenses them liberally. At some point, he dispenses with asking you things at all, you are simply be told what to do, and you do it or else.

He does not care what you think or how you feel. He does not care that you've kept all your promises and he's broken all of his. In his mind, he is the sole conferrer of rights and the sole possessor of authority in the relationship. As such, he has the power to allow or disallow your right to say "no". He is unaware of the unfairness of the imbalance of power in the relationship because it serves him to have the upper hand—this is how he lives. By this time, whatever you have with this man no longer resembles a marriage or a relationship. It is more like a train wreck in a prison yard.

9 Lovers Unmasked

Seeing Through the Masks

Moral dishonesty permeates everything an abuser does. His life, at core, is a sick sort of performance art. Some abusers mask their agenda very successfully in the beginning but do not maintain the guise for more than six months. Many abusive individuals are adept at wearing more than one mask, and within each persona there can be a great deal of variation.

One of the things that abusers have in common is that the man behind the mask, the man whose deceit requires the use of personas does not think there is anything questionable about his behavior. The other thing is his mental tally of his partner's transgressions. Part of the abusive mindset is retaliatory, and this is what he gets to indulge when the mask comes off.

The woman in an unhealthy relationship is stressed and oppressed, but often misunderstood because people outside the relationship believe the mask. Without knowledgeable support and without being able to learn how to see through the mask, she can't begin to understand the counter-intuitive world she's living in. She has no protection against the wiles of her abuser and she can sustain great psychological harm. She may have been so controlled and so unequipped to counter, that she comes to believe what her abuser tells her. The abusive partner acts one way in public, when he's wearing his mask and quite another when he's not.

The Animal Compassionate Mask

His abuse of animals foreshadows his abuse of you.

This man uses animals because he has observed that this is an effective way to attract and engage women. He leverages this association because it suggests that he is sensitive, kind, protective and possesses other appealing qualities. It also opens up the possibility of other kinds of shared activities and interests. In whatever context he presents himself, he uses animals to serve as a conduit through which he can connect with desirable women. The Animal Compassionate is not above sharing pictures of himself with animals that belong to someone else but without admitting that. He describes himself as animal-friendly, but he is not, he is animal indifferent. His animals, if he has any, tell another story. It is unfortunate when this type of individual actually has an animal, but this is the case when the animal is useful to him in the procurement of his prey. His animal(s) will be disengaged, timid or vicious.

He trades on the assumptions this mask affords him. It allows him to milk a sensitive persona while he delivers blows without ever raising his hand or his voice. He may employ the calm demeanor and quiet authority he's observed with animal trainers on you. He may even use hand signals! These "quiet" techniques become condescending quickly. They attach themselves like leeches to suck the life out of you. They can be every bit as bruising as blows to the physical body.

He acts out his sense of entitlement with animals because he can. There is no give and take—he demands compliance and punishes them severely when they fail to comply adequately. Most animals retreat in the face of pain and punishment, so life with an animal abuser masquerading as an Animal Compassionate is not a long or happy one.

He may indulge in cruelty to animals through rituals such as hunting or rodeo, or cruelty may be part of his everyday life because it is how he gets thing done. Callousness to animals is epidemic in "cowboy country" where animals are routinely overworked, underfed and left exposed to the elements. In some urban areas, animals are abused and killed in fighting and sacrificial rituals by the millions. Extreme animal abuse is a hallmark of psychopathy and moderate animal abuse demonstrates diminished capacity.

When you get involved with the Animal Compassionate, you may see the truth behind his mask in the lives of his animals before you see it in your own. The baseline of his treatment of animals occurs between neglect and abuse. You may witness extreme punishment and violence committed against them. If you try to intervene, he may turn on you. The mistreatment of animals witnesses his lack of compassion, his inability to accord respect and his lack of conscience.

He treats animals more like equipment than creatures with feelings.

He is covertly cruel or overtly savage with animals.

He "tries" to be patient with you, but not with your animals.

He becomes enraged over any consideration you give your animals as if it's an affront to him.

Predators go where there is prey. Animals, like children, are easy prey. Over 71 percent of family violence and domestic abuse cases involve long-standing animal abuse, too. Often, the abusive adult male as well as one or more of the children have become habituated to dealing with their anxiety by torturing animals for gratification. If you live with or marry an abusive man, you may observe that your once-friendly, well-adjusted animals avoid him or start misbehaving. Your animals may disappear, turn up with curious injuries or dead. You may also find that one or more of your children become abusive towards animals, which always leads to abuse of people.

As animal casualties occur, the Animal Compassionate may say he's sorry or he may not react. The truth is, he is pleased or relieved that something you care about has been hurt or removed. What he wants is for it to be just him and you, with nothing else to matter to you and nothing else to take your attention away from him. Ensure that your animals are protected. Do not delay in getting them to a safe place at the first sign of the potential for cruelty. Once he discerns what your animals mean to you, he will begin a campaign to separate you from them:

He may come up with logistical reasons, like wanting to travel a lot.

He may begin an emotional attack, like insinuating that you have an abnormal affection for or sexual attraction to your animals.

He proposes a deal, wherein if you give up your animals he will provide something he knows you want.

He does not hesitate to use your animals to control and manipulate you, and this may include killing them or taking them away without your knowledge. The run-up to a lethal solution could include offensive or sick accusations.

"You can be emotionally lazy with animals and that's why you have them."

"Your animals just stick around because you feed them."

"You have animals because you don't know how to relate to people—and you never will."

He twists your affection for your animals every way he can to break you down. In his mind, he may believe that your interest in your animals indicates lack of character and capacity for human relationships, namely with him. He may express this directly in words or deeds. You and your animals will suffer in ways that violate the dignity of life.

Mindset Principles

The principles at work underneath the Animal Compassionate mask express this mindset:
• Animals are his for the using
• They don't have feelings (they are "dumb" animals)
• If his woman cares about animals, she is defective and needs to be punished
• Animals are useful tools for manipulating people
• Seeing his partner or family upset over his torture of animals excites him
• He derives power from holding an animal's life in his hand and all the implications that holds for the people he is trying to control

Damaged boys often torment animals on their way to tormenting women. Many of the most heinous serial criminals began their "careers" torturing and killing animals. It's one thing to see your inanimate property lost, mishandled or destroyed. It's quite another to see your animals suffer and die without mercy at the hands of an abuser. When animals are at risk, so are people.

The Family Normalcy Mask

Beware of all agreements, spoken and unspoken, about children.

He knows children are the most powerful tools of all with which he can manipulate and control you and them. Like the Animal Compassionate, this guy professes a love of children. He does this to attract women because it gives him the appearance of being normal, stable and safe. If you have children, you can be sure he will use your love of your children to very great advantage—his.

He impregnates you to get himself into your life.

If you have small children, he uses their need of a daddy to compel you to marry or live with him.

If he has small children, he uses their need of a mommy to draw you in.

If he has grown children, they likely have serious issues of their own, which could adversely affect your wellbeing in the years to come.

If you marry this man, pay close attention to what provisions he makes for you and what provisions he makes for his children. Chances are you will be left out in the cold should you trust him to do the right thing. Even from the grave, he could abuse you.

Later, he may abuse or neglect your children. He may mistreat your children in front of you, but more likely he will do it when you're not around using techniques that do not leave a mark on the child, like shaking or suffocation. Do not allow this man unsupervised access to your children. It could cost them their lives. This happens every day.

Five million children witness the abuse of their mothers and thousands are killed themselves. If you cannot stick up for your children, get help from someone who will or get the children to a safe place and do this without delay.

He may impose rules on how you treat your own children.

He may threaten to kidnap or kill them.

He may concoct charges against you to have the state seize your children.

He may institute one set of rules for your children and one set for his.

He may try to coerce your children or his to testify against you in child custody hearings.

Mindset Principles

The principles at work underneath the Family Normalcy mask express this mindset:

• He believes his family exists to serve him, he is entitled to their primary allegiance

• His family is expected to cover his responsibilities and accept his excuses

• He is the head of the household and therefore always right

• If compliance is not forthcoming, it is incumbent upon him to dish out the appropriate punishment

• No one in the family can having anything in their life that matters more than him

One of the latest legal hurdles used against women by their abusers is the invocation of "parental alienation" actions. This is a claim that the effects of the mother's abuse have alienated the children from the abuser. This has now become a legal liability for the abused woman! A contest for child custody against an abuser may be the fight of your life. Because the Family Man has no conscience and is in denial about his abuse, none of this is hard for him to do and he has no remorse for his ill treatment of them or you.

The Wonderful Man Mask

Listen to what he says, but believe what he does. There are two sides to this man, a public side and a private side. His public side is well spoken, calm, reassuring, gentle; he is comfortable in his own, a man at peace with the world and with no need to prove anything to anyone. He has done it all. In conversation he is able to show interest and understanding. He is a master of drawing people out and making them feel special. He can call upon books, movies or news to suggest that he is informed and to punctuate his convictions about the issues of the day.

He plays the role of the gentleman to the hilt; he may even shed a tear to underscore his refinement and sensitivity. Not only do women fall for this, but so does everyone else. He fools her, her family, her friends, everyone. Although he doesn't appear to be calculated, his moves are well rehearsed and he never lets his mask slip in public. Later, when he begins to abuse her, she will doubt her sanity because of the gentleman mask he can don in the blink of an eye and because no one will believe what this gentleman is doing to his partner. The reality is that his public side bears little or no relation to his private side, which is abusive, unpredictable, cruel and threatening.

His behavior is emotionally dishonest and manipulative in both arenas. He is an ego-driven actor and an expert deceiver. This is part of why it's so hard to see his real self. When a woman doesn't know to look for a schism between his public and private side, she won't see his true nature until it's too late.

When people ask how you ever got involved with a man who later mistreated you, this is how: he played the role of the perfect gentleman for as long as it took to get you into his trap. Of course he didn't mistreat you at first. Abusers succeed because they have adopted winning ways, which they are able to maintain for limited periods of time. Setting up a relationship takes time and he knows that. Subconsciously he knows he has to entrap his victims with an act. He also knows he can get any victim he wants as long as he uses the right trap. The Wonderful Man knows if he dropped his act and revealed his private side too early, you would flee and he does not want you to get away.

His act is designed to draw you in.

His public self is one of easy-going self assurance.

His first impression is fabulous; his conduct unimpeachable.

He knows how to be charming and mannerly.

When he begins to be abusive, he will tell you that you are hurting him! Then he will enroll you in making it up to him, this will become an unwritten rule in the relationship which will be your burden for the duration, and which undermine the balance of power since you will be regularly put in the position of making it up to him. This rule will not apply to any hurt feelings you experience—double standards redux. Hurt feelings are all your fault. When he's not abusing you over his, he may put on his Wonderful Man mask and try to teach you how to "rise above it" or "do the right thing" or "think of someone besides yourself" for a change. Outside the closed doors, no one will be the wiser. The demeanor that charmed you in the beginning wins over everyone he meets. The older the abuser, the more convincing (and conniving) his game. He has no awareness of any trespass he commits against you; he wants your absolute adoration and undivided attention. He skillfully manipulates your perceptions of him to win your admiration. He acts humble, even self-effacing.

"I don't like to talk about myself."

"I don't take myself too seriously."

He leads you and everyone else to believe he is something other than what he really is—often the opposite.

He acts magnanimous when he is really petty.

He makes a show of generosity, when he is really miserly.

His plays a man of honor, when he is really dishonorable.

He paints pretty pictures with his words and promises you more than you ever asked for, when he really has no interest in your happiness and no intention of carrying through on his promises—any of them.

"I just want to make you happy."

"You deserve this and so much more."

"I want to be everything to you."

Take note of his persona. His public self reveals a lot about who and what he thinks himself to be. This is how he functions in society. It is an expertly crafted persona that is attractive and appealing. This is who his co-workers, neighbors and others in the community know him to be. This type of man knows exactly what buttons to push. He knows what to say and how to say it. His delivery has perfect pitch. This is because he has been refining his method for most of his life.

Mindset Principles

The principles at work underneath this mask express these attitudes:

"I'm above the coarseness of life and petty squabbles, I would never do anything base."

"I am a desirable man. I know it and women know it, so take good care of me because men like me don't come along often."

"I expect to be catered to, noblesse oblige and all that, you know.

"I understand you better than you understand yourself and I expect you to respond to the things I tell you in this regard."

"I have a lot of experience with women so I know more than you do and you would be wise to take my advice."

The eventual revelation of his real character will be in sharp contrast to his perfect gentleman act. He may be getting ready to deliver his coup de grace on you.

The All-Around Guy Mask

He has a lot of acquaintances, but no friends.

His social interactions are all highly choreographed so that he can gain the upper hand in every exchange. He may initiate all such activities with flattery, extraordinary friendliness or magnanimous posturing to charm and disarm the other person. It is like a game to him and he plays it without inhibition because he knows it well.

He is cunning in how he presents himself to people. Despite his studied assertions to the contrary, this man is highly preoccupied with achieving advantage, promoting his image and elevating his position.

Nothing that he does is out of regard for anyone but himself. He is self-serving to an extreme degree.

- He name drops.
- He attends church.
- He makes appearances.
- He flaunts his resources.
- He indulges his desires.

The type of person he presents himself to be may give you clues to his capabilities as an intimate partner. It may tell you things about the nature of his childhood and his familial relations. It may explain things to you about other aspects of his life now, or later. For example, he may tell you emphatically that he's from a great family, has great relationships with his parents and children. However, you may not witness anything to confirm these claims and you may very well later learn that this is all completely false. You may also observe that the entire family participates in this charade.

He is often formulaic with people. He greets different people the same way, such as with a hearty handshake, a clap on the back, or some show of over-friendliness. Depending on how well he's known, if you look carefully, you may see cracks in his veneer.

You may see people visibly put off by him.

You may see he is always more animated than the people he talks to.

You may also see they move away first.

When you go out with him, you never know if it is going to be a normal, peaceful outing or not. When he's in a mood, you find yourself more or less abandoned while he drinks, talks loudly, hits on other women and so forth. You'll be ignored except for dirty looks from across the room. When the event is over, he may seethe in silence or unload on you in the car on the way home. In either case, you're in trouble because of something you did or did not do. And this transgression of yours is his excuse for whatever he decides to do to you afterwards.

Mindset Principles

The principles at work underneath the All-Around Guy mask express this mindset:

• He is not responsible for his actions because he is such a great all around guy

• His woman should be grateful to be with him, anything less is unacceptable

• His reputation sets him apart, entitles him and belongs to him forever

• Anyone who can't see what a great guy he is, is an idiot and not to be tolerated

Being told off—told how to behave, threatened on the way to or berated on the way home from outings—becomes part of your life. No matter how social you once were, you find yourself anticipating public outings with equal parts longing and dread. When it's too late to matter, you may realize that the friends he has talked up and talked about were friends from long ago or from another part of the country. These people may be clueless about his true nature, which is worse now than it was when he knew them.

The Lady-Killer Mask

Feeling sorry for him because of his "proclivities" is a trap.

This guy leads with zest for life, which is often wrapped in an appealing mix of energy, libido and ego. This is an effortless mask for the psychopath to wear because it gives him free rein to indulge himself—his favorite thing. It lets him be insatiable, immature, youthful and self-centered. The beginning of an intrigue with him can be mesmerizing because it plays to the woman's sense of fun with lots of partying, adventuring, lovemaking, etc. The fun she has will make her fall for this man harder and faster than she would without the excitement factor.

He is the type of man who can make every activity compelling and spectacular. He can make a woman feel very special by including her in his "exciting" and "extraordinary" daily existence. He traffics in fun, but when it comes to anything else, like commitment or exclusivity, he starts back-peddling. If you can see through the haze, you'll see that his devotion to fun is really devotion to himself because it draws on his selfishness, lack of control, denial, minimizing and sneaking or lying (substance abuse).

When he overindulges in his substance of choice and then abuses you, you may think there's a connection between the two, but there's not. Abusive people don't abuse because they're drunk or stoned, they abuse because they're abusive. Their altered state is just a convenient excuse and something they can use to appeal to your compassion or patience. Altering substances function as disinhibitors, but they are not the cause of abuse, the cause is something far deeper than blood alcohol. He may believe there's a connection between his partying and his bad behavior, but his belief is not substantiated by research.

Drinking and drug use alter perception and introduce a torpor and surrealism that comes from chemical imbalance. It allows him to keep from facing himself and his behavior. Chemical alteration only deepens the individual and collective quicksand you're already in. There are numerous risks you face in dealing with this guy. His substance use heightens all forms of his risky behavior, such as driving, spending money and physical or sexual assault.

When you see his fun seeking intensify, you'll also see his level of interest wane; his attention will begin to wander. The chances of being in an exclusive relationship with him are nil, he just doesn't work that way, no matter what he says. Remember, he lives by distraction and thrill seeking. Chances are the Lady Killer is playing you like he's played others, taking things as far as he can to squeeze every last drop of "fun" out of each involvement.

If you are a woman who can't see the writing on the wall and tries to "stand by her man" you will soon find that your formerly fascinating romantic partner—except when he wants his needs met—is able to treat you with great callousness. If you stick around after this revelation, your self image is going to take a beating. If you try to weather his playing the field in spite of everything you are doing to keep him "satisfied" and at home, you are in for disappointment and possibly violence because you are, in fact, dealing with an abusive and immature man who doesn't care about anyone but himself. You face the most risk when you catch him in the act or confront him with evidence of cheating. Another risk is getting enrolled in fun seeking with him by drinking, taking drugs or engaging in other thrill seeking activities.

It's important to understand that:

• Getting him off the bottle (or whatever) will not eradicate the problems in the relationship because alcohol (or whatever) is not the root cause of his abuse of you.

• Getting him off the bottle will only reduce the substance-related excuses he can draw on to justify his behavior. If he gets off the bottle, be assured, he will find other ways to excuse his abuse of you.

He has considerable charm and expertise in keeping you focused on his enjoyment rather than focusing on what you need to do to protect yourself from the consequences of being involved with him. He may even claim he wants to reform in order to string you along for a little while longer.

Mindset Principles

The principles at work underneath this mask express this mindset:

- Life is short and he deserves every good thing he can avail himself of
- Exclusivity is too limiting
- His fun seeking should be supported
- He can't help it if he overdoes it (alcohol, drugs, sex, etc.)

Yet another pitfall you face in dealing with the Lady Killer is eventually using fun seeking behaviors yourself, such as alcohol or drugs, as a means of distraction or self medicating to help you cope with being abused.

The Technologist Mask

In the wired realm, there are no consequences and no accountability— a psychopath's wet dream.

This guy is connected to electronics all day and much of the night. If he is young, he is addicted to video games, surfing the web, texting his friends. If he is in the work force, he is addicted to his work, the news, pornography, games, etc. If he grew up addicted to electronics (pornography, video games, horror films), by the time he was 18, he had been exposed to about a quarter million images of violence, including 50 thousand scenes of murder. These electronic entertainments are calibrated to engage and arouse. The result of this "formula" is virtual, not really felt. This is dangerous territory in which the perpetrator acts with impunity no matter what he does to his victim(s). Without real consequence there is no psychological impact, no emotional reckoning, no opportunity to think about what is being done to the victim.

He tends to grow up not to taking anything too seriously, including life and death. He probably had a "NO FEAR" bumper sticker on his first car. When you don't feel emotions, fear is one of them.

Unfortunately, some of the best paying jobs happen to be most technological and the best selling entertainments happen to be the most violent. Being immersed in the virtual world blurs the distinction between the real and the unreal, accountability and unaccountability. It also retards personal growth and social development. It is no secret that high tech has its own culture, and one of its characteristics is the absence of social skills. When this is intensified by abuse, the effects on you can be terrifying. When you are compromised by an inadequate self image, you may endure mistreatment for years.

He spends his waking hours in front of his electronic device(s).

He interrupts any activity with you to take a call, check email, etc.

He may spend inordinate amounts of money on hardware, software, memberships and subscriptions that allow him greater access to his preferred gratifications.

He becomes enraged when anyone suggests that he "put that thing down" or "turn that thing off."

When he does disconnect, he is distracted, sullen, wrathful until he gets back in front of his device. During the last two decades of the 20th century, 15 billion dollars was spent by consumers on electronic entertainments, a high number of which contained graphical depictions of violence. These were (and are) amplified; that is, violent acts are rendered as more gruesome rather than more realistic. Over time, this does things to the human mind. Based on neuroscience, interactive engagement exerts greater influence. As he becomes more sophisticated, he becomes capable of doing more damage.

Mindset Principles

The principles at work underneath the Technologist mask express this mindset:

• He is accustomed to acting with the impunity he has in the virtual world no matter what he does to his victim

• He does not need to develop personally to excel in the virtual world, he does not want to do this for his partner either

• He is capable of over-the-top abuse because his wiredness removes the reality of consequences

• He does not think twice about using his technological expertise to sabotage or destroy his partner

• When his victim tries to leave him, he cyber stalks her

An addiction to violent electronic media is a red flag in bullying, teen dating abuse, domestic violence, animal torture, elder abuse and political tyranny. It does not just depend on the neurological subsets of psychopathy but conveys its own dulling of right and wrong.

The Misunderstood Man Mask

He has an insatiable need for attention, nurturing and sympathy; these needs are placed, along with his head, in the lap of his victim.

He uses tales of woe to play upon the emotions of this victim. He engages his prey by making a first impression that shows and tells how he has been overlooked, disrespected, impoverished, abused (!), wronged and violated by others. His story may be large or small. It may center on the treatment he supposedly received by his ex-girlfriend or ex-wife or it may encompass his entire life. His purpose in crafting this tale is to find women who are not only highly compassionate, but gullible, naive and maternal. He wants to be relieved of it all.

He blames any of his own limitations, such as being broke, unemployed, on the run and so forth on persecution by others.

What he doesn't say, but what his victim will eventually find out is that he considers his status as persecuted to be his ticket to ride and his blanket excuse.
The stories that he comes up with to snow women comprise the laughable, the impressive and everything in-between.

His wounds can be real or imagined.

They may derive from a difficult childhood, poor health (addiction, injury, disease), financial loss, emotional distress, spiritual torment and more. His stories can be based on something factual and then enlarged to suit his needs or they may be entirely fabricated. The most effective stories are those that contain at least one fact that can be demonstrated—this small bit of truth is often enough to enroll the victim, who needs no further evidence of his woundedness because she is falling for his other ploys, especially his charms and promises.

He is most successful with women who don't know his history and are not likely to find out about it.

If he is an adept abuser, he has covered his tracks with great care by moving, changing jobs, making strategic changes to his appearance, preying on women in another locale, etc.

If he has resources and is out for highly desirable prey, he can alter or remove records and construct an elaborate structure to give just the right appearance to support his persona.

There is perhaps no caretaking and relief of responsibility that would be too much for him. When his victim begins to weary of the burden of his unending need—which can go on for months or years if he has chosen well—he wraps his abuse in inversion and projection:

• when she objects or resists, he accuses her of being "just like all the others" who have treated him so unfairly

• when she expresses the wish that he could get on his feet or rise above his past, he accuses her of doing to him what he is doing to her—using and abusing—when in fact, she is not

These techniques give the abuser a way to tighten controls and gain more ground while also setting up the victim to feel more defective, obligated and guilty.

Mindset Principles

The principles at work underneath this mask express this mindset:

• He has suffered great wrongs and is therefore entitled to unending loyalty and support

- The abuses he has endured make him unassailable because he is the perennial victim, which state he milks ad nauseum
- He should be allowed to do whatever he wants to do without question or limitation because of all that he has suffered
- He is unconstrained in his predations because he is blameless and anyone who thinks otherwise is out to get him

Like all pathological abusers, the Misunderstood Man is empty and blameless. His mistreatment by others when he is such a blameless, innocent, righteous man can compound the emotional ammunition and penetrate even the most sophisticated heart with the seamless lying that only a psychopath can deliver.

10 Harvey and Claire

They met in the airport on a day when winter had
unleashed its fury on Denver. Claire was flying back to
Stanford after the holidays with her family in Boston.
Harvey was flying back to Harvard from seeing friends
in Portland. Their flights had been canceled; there were
no rooms at the inn. They took separate refuge in a back
corner of an all-night restaurant. After a quarter hour of
talking across two tables, Claire invited Harvey to join
her. The food was awful, but they were ravenous, so
they ate. They talked, laughed, read, relaxed and talked
some more. They walked up and down the long
gateways. His presence was comfortable and it protected
her from unwanted attention. She marveled at how a
stranger, although a nice one, could make her feel so
much at ease and self assured.

They worked through the usual topics without rush—the
weather, the economy, their studies. Then they told
some of their own stories as the hours passed and
reserve gave way to connection. Claire grew up slow,
good and a little neglected. A dutiful child, by the time
she was 10 years old she could run a household by
herself, except for driving to the grocery store. She once
heard her mother praise her character to her
grandmother on the phone. Her heart rose and she
determined to live up to it. She grew into a responsible,
serious, kind and tenacious woman. Harvey on the other
hand, had weathered one tragedy after another in his
early years. His family had died in a house fire when he
was seven. Over the next nine years, he'd lived with all
six of his aunts and uncles and his 11 cousins. Nothing

had lasted for long somehow. He had not grown up poor, but he had grown up without the intangible things that make people a family.

"Inadequately loved," Claire thought as she listened to his matter-of-fact reportage while they walked and talked.

When her flight was finally rescheduled for the afternoon, she realized she felt a pang about their parting. Their last few hours were filled with animate dialogue and self disclosure. At the last minute, they made their way to Claire's flight gate. They regarded each other with liquid eyes and exchanged email addresses while the queue to board formed. He took her hand, closed his around hers and squeezed. He wished her a good trip, said he'd be in touch and then stepped back. She smiled, nodded and without meaning to, sighed out loud. They both laughed. Then he turned on his heel and walked away from the boarding area. When her plane touched down in San Francisco she was still savoring the feel of his hand around hers. She thought about his hand, his face and the things he'd said until she fell asleep in her bed a few hours later.

His first email landed in her Inbox just before midnight four days later. She was overjoyed and relieved, almost to the point of tears, which surprised her. They emailed, talked on the phone and Skyped with increasing frequency until it became part of daily life. Claire would be graduating with her B.F.A. that May, Harvey with his J.D. in June. By February, they were talking about meeting somewhere in June. By March, they had decided to meet halfway and spend spring break together in the Smokey Mountains.

It was five days of soul knitting—they talked non-stop or they didn't need words. The days passed in a sort of heightened animation, they existed apart from the world. They walked the hills by day and explored each other's hearts and minds by firelight. The night before they flew back to their respective lives, Harvey came up behind her as she did dishes in the cabin's tiny sink. "Not ready to go."

"I know. Me, neither."

He reached down, pulled her left hand out of the water, then slipped a band of diamonds and rubies on her ring finger. She stood transfixed gazing at the ring on her wet hand. He stepped away from her, turned his palms up and laughed saying, "Well? Do I have to get down on one knee?"

She came to, spun on the balls of her feet and threw her arms around him. He folded her in his arms and she melted into him. They held each other and let the moment sink in. In-between his kisses and the images of their future that flitted through her mind's eye, she wondered how her parents would take the news. The suddenness was intoxicating.

Her parents could hear it in her voice and were glad she was so happy, but not enamored of such a quick engagement. What was the big rush they wanted to know? She was 22. He was 28. They were just getting started. Did they have to take this step so soon? They had their whole lives before them—exactly what she'd expected. So, she brought him home for inspection. Over a long weekend of spring storms that kept them inside too much, she sat and watched as one-by-one, he won them over—without even trying. He entered their home as a stranger and left it as a new member of the family. At the door, he picked Claire up off her feet in a big bear hug and kissed her on the forehead. Then, he looked each of her parents in the eye, took their hand and said a few words to them. Just before the final good-bye, he bent down and gave her mother a kiss on the back of her hand. Her mother sighed out loud and her dad put his arm around his wife as if to catch her in a swoon. Claire and Harvey exchanged a look and then he ran down to the taxi waiting at the curb.

The next five months went by in a blur. They graduated and began interviewing all over the country. Once they got a chance to coordinate interviews so they could meet in the same town. On a rendezvous in Taos, they picked a date and decided to move to the first place where one of them was offered a good job. They had a small wedding that September in Boston with her family and friends.

They drove up the coast and explored coastal Maine for a week. They met in an airport, got engaged in a cabin, married in an old chapel and honeymooned on a storm-tossed coast, all in less than a year. They had their first disagreement on the drive back to Boston. Harvey wanted Claire to change some social plans when they got back. She didn't want to and said "no" never dreaming it would become a thing. It was nothing, she thought. She'd never seen him behave this way. He wasn't about to give way and she lost heart at the hostility that rose up in him, so she relented. The rest of the drive passed in silence. She thought about it for days, running things over and over in her head without making sense of any of it. They never spoke about the thing again.

She moved into his apartment and put her job search on a back burner while his went into high gear. She packed boxes every day in anticipation of a move. Neither of them wanted to stay in Boston and she had a gut feeling they would soon be off to a new beginning. On a trip to Chicago, he took a position with a large law firm. Several of the managing partners took him out to dinner with two other new hires and kept them out half the night. One of the new hires was a flashy redhead without a wedding band. It was the first evening that he did not call his wife.

Thanks to Claire's packing, they made quick work of the move. The air was turning cold when they began their new life in the windy city. Harvey threw himself into his work. Claire unpacked, set up the apartment and then resumed her own search for work. She explored the city by herself. She ate dinner at home alone and missed her husband. Harvey worked late most evenings and one or both days many weekends. He said it was what all new hires were expected to do. When he was home, he said he was tired. If he talked to her, it sounded like he was talking to a subordinate. When she pointed this out, he'd shrug his shoulders or laugh, but he never apologized and he didn't quit using that tone of voice with her. He always showered at night, but even so, on the infrequent mornings when they made love, she began to notice that his body smelled different. Many nights, she lay beside him in the dark feeling alone. Something that she loved very much seemed to have gone out of him and she ached for it. Twice she thought of leaving him and going back to Newport or Palo Alto. Both times, he seemed to sense her retreat and the old Harvey animated him for a few hours or a few days. She hung on to those hours and days.

Her job search became a chore; she called on her resolve and persistence to keep on. Her despondency over her invisible husband seemed to suck the marrow out of her bones. She had never been through such a peculiar passage—she wanted it to be over so they could have the marriage they'd envisioned that night in the cabin, which seemed like a lifetime ago. It was winter in her soul and in the art world, too, it seemed. About the time she felt too dispirited to keep on; she got a job. She immersed herself in the work and began to take comfort in the new routine, although not much at home was comforting. She worked as a liaison between artists and customers in one of the oldest galleries in Chicago. She worked on the floor a bit, but mostly she met with artists and called on the gallery's coveted list of discerning art patrons of high net worth.

Harvey continued his over-achieving ways at the law firm talking his way through one case after another, impressing clients and associates alike. He demonstrated an uncanny ability to get people to show their hand at just the right moment or else withhold key information that later sank them. He was moving up in the estimation of those whose estimation mattered to his future.

He had made himself into the sort of man who made things happen and moved fast. The redhead would tell him the same thing at their hotel room on Tuesday evenings—he moved fast. She had no idea. This was who he was, and each of the women with whom he had sexual congress in various rooms around the city—if it was more than a one-night stand—eventually said more or less the same thing. "Naked aggression" was another response he got and he like that one a lot. On the contrary, his sex life with Claire was unremarkable.

On one of their first assignations, the redhead had brought a little flask of brandy and a line of cocaine for them to share. Harvey felt his blood turn into rocket fuel and his member into a fuselage. It was better than looking at pornography. He began to search for other substances that did the same thing, but wouldn't get in the way at work. With careful procurement and disciplined experimentation, he found a number and used them with superhuman precision.

On their anniversary, Harvey added a few grains of one of his favorite "enhancers" to Claire's coffee and brought it to her along with breakfast in bed. He knew she would be delighted by his gesture and compliant the rest of the day. In the course of his twenties, Harvey had perfected the Emotional Diet. Most days, he gave Claire very little to subsist on, then he would give her a feast and watch with amusement as she fed hungrily on whatever emotional sustenance he presented. He believed this was one of the keys to keeping a woman in line and at home.

They ate breakfast in bed, lounged, read the paper and planned their day. Since it was their anniversary, Claire wanted to see some of the sights with him, go out to dinner and then to a movie. He let her pick their destinations and nodded in approval with each one she proposed. She did not know that he had already seen the sights and had nice dinners with dozens of young beauties while she sat home alone.

He watched her become almost giddy like a girl. He watched her over the newspaper and when he saw her pupils begin to dilate, he rose and walked into the bathroom for a quick shower. He left the door open knowing she would watch him step out of his boxers. He was also feeling the effects and would be showing them momentarily. He took his time in the shower and gave Claire every eyeful he could without giving himself away.

By the time he walked back into bedroom, she was sitting on the edge of the bed. Her cheeks were flushed; he thought she looked adorable in a way he hadn't seen for a while. She also felt urgent. Wrapped in a towel he stood at the window a few feet away from the end of the bed as if to assess the weather. She crawled across the covers, ran her hand up his thigh and the games began. She pulled him down on the bed and was on him like a cat. He knew he was about to see Claire unleashed and he was well prepared. The thing about his magic dust was that he needed very little time in-between climaxes to mount a new effort. He got up to leave the bed only to have Claire dart across the room, pull him down on the chaise, arch her back like a bow and vocalize like he had never heard before. As expected, she was childlike and uninhibited. Her lack of sexual restraint amused him as he mentally compared it with it what he'd experienced with the other women he'd treated to his magic dust and then his big, handsome self.

Instead of exploring Chicago together, they had sex all day long at home. They moved around the apartment, draping themselves on soft surfaces and fed on each other. He knew to pace himself, Claire did not. He let her be voracious with him, watching with cool objectivity as she pleasured him and herself. He performed with enormous energy and deft timing, making her pause or slow down until she whimpered, then giving his all when she was at the point of frenzy. By evening, Claire had friction marks all over her hips and torso but she didn't seem to mind. They ate, went back in the bedroom and fell asleep. They awoke after dark. He felt good—rested and spent at the same time. Claire was happy, a little sore, but still game. They had some brandy at a table in the den with a view of the city, then walked back to the bedroom, watched TV and went to sleep. This became a regular ritual.

In his second year with the firm, Harvey was approached by a client to take a complicated case for which he would be handsomely paid—if he took it off the books. The terms were irresistible, so he took it. The work was arduous and required extra help from his black-market pharmacy, but he continued to hit the mark with his day job and with the secret case. Within a month of finalizing it, another one was proffered with a bigger, richer pot. He lost 20 pounds doing it, but thanks to his little helpers, he over delivered and began to feel invincible.

One night at a five-star hotel, a little Latina brought more than he bargained for. Before the drugs and sex, she read his cards. After sex, they played with the Ouija board. He noted the difference in her demeanor. In bed, her passion was ethereal; with the cards and the board, it was all business. He didn't take any of it seriously, except getting off, which he did with great power.

Claire continued to drift along in the marriage. She had made a place for herself at the gallery although the rest of her existence felt pale. She couldn't make up her mind whether she didn't like Chicago or she didn't like her marriage. Harvey provided a sort-of life for her.

When he was home, he wasn't really present or else he smothered her. He was alternately hostile and sweet, which kept her walking on eggshells and wondering what to do. She lived for their weekends together, even though the pharmaceutically-fueled sex games were growing old. Once she caught on that he'd been giving her something, she demanded that he stop, which he did, along with any interest in their sex life. There had to be more to marriage than having coffee in the morning, keeping house and sharing drugged sex.

Harvey had the Latina once a week, then twice a week, then three times a week—far more than any other woman, including the redhead, who he'd used up long before. He began to pay attention to more than her body parts and over the summer, they actually spent more time bent over the coffee table looking at the cards or the board or his palm. Sometimes she would chant and howl. Eventually, she required blood and semen, which he provided without hesitation. Once she smeared him with feces in the bathroom. Their sex became guttural and animalistic. He felt like a god as he bored into her and she screeched with sensation.

He recorded some of their sessions and listened to them over and over. He thought at length about the things she said and began to apply them to see what would happen. Each private little experiment gave him a rush and delivered some new gift to him. He was so well pleased with himself that he strutted around Chicago in a state of semi-arousal. At first, he hid it with his outerwear, but eventually he decided he did not need to hide it. When women noticed, most of them would look away, but some of them would lock eyes with him, confirming his powers. One woman opened her blouse on a long elevator ride, they skipped their floors, went up to the roof and tore into each other on the stair landing. Without meaning to, he strangled her. It hardly made the news. "The anonymity of the big city," he chuckled to himself.

He knew he had crossed a line and that nothing he wanted would be withheld. The Latina never said so, but Harvey came to the conclusion that he was at a jumping off place and it was time to free himself of the amateurs he worked with and the bland woman he lived with because none of them were worthy and wanted to grow with him.

He became emboldened enough to resign his job so he could work exclusively with his back-door clients. He was paid huge sums of money, most of which never landed in domestic bank accounts. He replaced his salary, but put the rest of it in foreign accounts. He received payment in drugs and women, too. He devoured all of it. At this rate, he would be able to retire by 40. He had bought a stone mansion with terraced grounds above the coast of Croatia for that very reason. On their fourth anniversary, Harvey did not come home until midnight. Claire had cancelled their dinner reservation and gone to bed hungry, but otherwise numb. She was done and would tell him so in the morning. She fell asleep mid-prayer. She did not hear him come in the front door, but she did hear him moving around in the living room and kitchen. She had no desire to get up. Things got quiet; she assumed he'd crashed on the sofa in the den, so she began to drift off. Sometime later, she woke up to see Harvey standing over her. She moved to switch on the lamp at the exact moment he

bent down and scooped her up in his arms like a baby.
"What?" was all she said.

He kissed her on the forehead, but didn't say a word, he
just smiled that smile. He carried her through the
luxurious apartment. In the den, she saw two brandy
snifters and a wrapped box on the game table. She
thought he'd prepared a nightcap and brought her an
anniversary present. She looked up at him, but he was
looking at their reflection in the sliding glass door. He
put her hand on him, he was hard. He carried her like
she weighed no more than a child. He nuzzled her neck
and opened the door. She folded her arms over her chest
and looked into his eyes not knowing what she was
seeing and wondering if the man she'd married was
coming back to her. She expected to be lowered onto
one of the lounge chairs to make love in the moonlight.
He held her gaze and squeezed her lightly. Without
letting her drop her gaze, he took four strides across the
balcony, held her out and spread his arms wide as she
dropped through the air. The last thing he saw in the dim
light was a look of disbelief beginning to form on her
face.

If her nightgown had not caught on hardware for a
hanging flower box, she would have fallen 29 floors.
Instead she slid down the overhang as she came out of
her gown and dropped naked onto the edge of the
balcony below. She fell to the floor and scooted toward
the building, but did not make another move. She
cupped her hands over her mouth and willed herself to
be silent. She could hear Harvey walking back and forth
above and wondered what he could see of the ground
below. At length, he went inside and closed the glass
door behind him.

Claire did not know onto whose balcony she had landed. She wanted to get up and bang on the door, but decided it was safer to hide until morning. She crawled to a door at one end and went inside the storage room to get out of the night chill. She found a tablecloth and wrapped herself in it. She sank to the floor, drew her knees up and put her head on her arms. She turned her head to the side tasting her own blood and sweat on her arm, and feeling no small amount of deliverance.

Afterword

The overlay between the psychopathic and the possessed is staggering. The major distinction is the supernatural repertoire of the possessed (the ability to mind-read, levitate, speak in other languages, move objects, exert superhuman strength).

The psychopath and the possessed are driven to destroy. The psychopath is driven by the absence of conscience, the possessed is driven by the presence of hatred; the actions of both embody evil and if unchecked, leads to the annihilation of their victim.

Is the reality of men abusing women another symptom of the present moral decay or has it always existed along the darkest psychological fringes of society? I do not know.

The information in this book has helped Donna's recovery and our family's ability to get our heads around her experience and what it means. It has been a wake-up call for each of us in different ways. We are all become more conscious in our relationships and we are reaping unexpected dividends in that department.

Time will tell what measure of discernment this information has cultivated in the minds of our children as they begin to date and learn about emotional intimacy. They have no public role models and few non-public ones.

Speaking for the men in our family, I can say this: any man who mistreats his woman (child or animal) in front of one of us will find he has opened up a can of whoop-ass on himself the likes of which he has never known. In reading dozens and dozens of stories about abuse, the element that was absent in nearly every one was a helpful man. Where are the brothers, fathers, sons, cousins, neighbors of all these abused women? How can they look away? How can they look themselves in the eye?

You would never know what Donna has been through to look at her or watch her interact with people, except for the fact, that she has not allowed another man into her life yet. She does not hate men or fear them, but outside family and childhood friends, she does not trust them yet. This is another consequence that follows that of falling prey to a predator—the long period of self-imposed exile while the heart, mind and spirit heal.

How many women never have children because their recovery occurs during their final fertile years? How many women never recover the financial losses they sustained from abuse?

As many people on the planet are guided into the baser pursuits of ever more primitive and secular interests, evil continues to prevail with predictable success. The careless and the uninformed—no matter how accomplished, good looking, well educated or financially secure—continue to be at great risk.